Strangers in a Strange Church?

New Faces of Ukrainian Catholicism in Canada

Christopher Guly

Introduction by Fr. Peter Galadza
of the Sheptytsky Institute of Eastern Christian Studies,
University of St. Michael's College
in the University of Toronto

NOVALIS

© 2019 Novalis Publishing Inc.

Cover design and layout: AudreyWells
Cover image: istockphoto
Interior photographs courtesy of the subjects of the book.

Published by Novalis

Publishing Office
1 Eglinton Avenue East, Suite 800
Toronto, Ontario, Canada
M4P 3A1

Head Office
4475 Frontenac Street
Montréal, Québec, Canada
H2H 2S2

www.novalis.ca

Cataloguing in Publication is available from Library and Archives Canada.
ISBN: 978-2-89688-747-7

Printed in Canada.

We acknowledge the support of the Government of Canada.

5 4 3 2 1   23   22   21   20   19

Contents

Dedication

To Fr. Robert Anderson (+2003) and Fr. Michael Winn,
fellow "strangers" who have helped guide other "outsiders,"

and

To the "cradle" Ukrainian Greco-Catholics –
and their spouses – who in diverse ways made the first steps
of the transition easier:

Fr. Terry and Lada Cherwick
Fr. Andriy and Halyna Chirovsky
Larisa and Kenneth Cronin
Fr. Roman and Irene Galadza
Olenka, Daniel, Marika and Ivanka Galadza
Paul and Alexandra Kozak
Fr. Roman Lahola
Juliette Marczuk
Deacon Brad Moleski
Melita Mudri-Zubacz
Fr. Cyril Mykytiuk OSBM
Fr. Roman and Lilya Rytsar
Cassandra Thompson
Christina Thompson
Gloria and Harvey Winn
Fr. Stephen and Maria Wojcichowsky
Vera Yuzyk
Walter and Marianne Zubrycky

Special thanks to Daniel Bezalel Richardsen
for his guidance in seeing this "dream publication" come true.

Introduction

A title like *Strangers in a Strange Church?* probably requires some explaining. To begin with, note the question mark. It's rhetorical. The nine people described here are not foreigners in the Ukrainian Greco-Catholic Church (UGCC),[1] nor is their Church strange. Of course, some people of Ukrainian background have considered or continue to consider these non-Ukrainians "outsiders." And certainly many North Americans view the UGCC – like most Eastern Churches – as exotic. However, that's what makes these stories so compelling. They document struggle and success.

The book narrates the lives of seven individuals and one couple who have joined the UGCC in Canada, more specifically Ottawa, in the last 25 years. None of them is of Ukrainian background, but they are among the best "Ukrainian" Catholics I've ever met. They're all young and they are all passionate about living a Christian lifestyle. The combination of youth and commitment to Jesus Christ – according to an Eastern tradition that many Ukrainian Canadians themselves have jettisoned – is beguiling.

In addition to being entirely of non-Ukrainian background, all of the people whose stories are told here have two other things in common: their faith formation took place in or via other faith communities, and in diverse ways they have all given back to their new community – not to mention the world at large. As regards

---

1 "Ukrainian Greco-Catholic" is technically the more accurate name of the Church. The elimination of "Greco-" became common in English because греко-католик (*hreko-katolyk)* was almost always mistakenly rendered as "Greek Catholic," which added confusion to perplexity. But "Greco-Catholic" has a far stronger pedigree than "Ukrainian Catholic." In Ukraine, until the early 1990s, the former was the Church's sole name. In fact, today in Ukraine, "Ukrainian Catholic" (without "Greco-") refers to the Church of the Roman, not Eastern, rite. However, in the present publication we follow the convention that took hold in Western countries after World War II. Prior to that period, the term "Ruthenian Greek-Catholic Church" was usually employed throughout the West. With the painful loss of Ukrainian statehood twice in one generation and the evolution of national consciousness, the Vatican acceded to the Ukrainian diaspora's popular demand for the change in nomenclature.

the first: these nine individuals were raised Evangelical, Roman-rite Catholic, Anglican, Pentecostal and Salvation Army. The Ukrainian Greco-Catholic Church is thus the beneficiary of an evangelization and faith formation that took place elsewhere. But this book is not about proselytism. (More on that below.)

As for giving back to the UGCC: within their adopted communities, these newcomers have taken on vital roles. They supervise the local youth group; they volunteer with the UGCC monthly soup-kitchen initiative; they serve on the parish council; they have revitalized their church's catechetical program. Some have even become energetic members of the local Ukrainian Council of the Knights of Columbus! One of them, Lisa Gilbert, also dares to dream. She is the only one of the nine who presently lives outside Canada. Having moved to Kansas, where she attends an Antiochene Orthodox church for vespers and a Roman Catholic church for Mass, she wistfully asserts: "There was once a Ukrainian Catholic mission [in Wichita]. Perhaps I'm [here] to try to get the mission parish started up again!"

Regarding work in the world at large, the group includes a former civil servant who has championed the cause of religious freedom from Indonesia to Crimea (Andrew Bennett); a physician who risked her life to serve in Ebola-stricken West Africa (the above-mentioned Lisa Gilbert); and soccer parents (Rebecca and Harold Visser) who have bravely defied a football league establishment to help immigrant children avoid the street. Even with seven children of their own, the couple has enabled Muslim and Christian youths from Somalia, Syria and Latin America to obtain affordable membership in local soccer clubs.

Paradoxically, it is these non-Ukrainians who bolster Ukrainian secular life as well. The former Baptist of Goan-Indian background (Brian Butcher) becomes the cantor at prayer services for Ukraine on Parliament Hill. His children, along with those of other "converts," form a phalanx of volunteers at Ottawa's Ukrainian festival, and it is they who – owing to their musical talent – are called upon to sing the Ukrainian national anthem at Ottawa City Hall on

Ukrainian Independence Day! Their acceptance by "super-Ukes" has sometimes been tortuous. But this, too, is an edifying story – a testimony to how fresh blood, pulsating with a sincere love for Christ, can cleanse the wounds of ethnic inbreeding. Indeed, scores of cradle Ukrainian Catholics have come to embrace these newcomers as heroic "recruits."

These stories thus testify to the power of an Eastern Christian spiritual tradition that is deeply embedded in the Gospel – and surprisingly effective even in post-Christian Canada. It is the story of Christians whose roots lie elsewhere, but whose authentic Christianity has helped them appreciate this Eastern tradition in all its profundity. Fasting, intense prayer, constant study and sacrificial service typify this depth. And the newcomers' passion for forging new relationships with others has helped expose those who actually are of Ukrainian ancestry to the deep, rather than simply folkloric, grounding of their own Ukrainian spiritual Tradition.

Several more explanatory notes are apropos. Initially, I had wanted to write this book myself. These "strangers" have not only bolstered my faith in the living God but have inspired me to remain committed to my Church at moments when doing so was exasperating, to say the least. (More on that below.) However, coming from my pen, the book would have been hagiography. That's how much I revere these people. And while I personally may be a fan of the *vitae* genre, it doesn't sell very well. Besides, the "saints" described here would have been the first to object. They abhor anything that draws attention to themselves. Providentially, Chris Guly, a superb veteran journalist, became interested in them, and the rest is history.

One may wonder, "Why just these nine – and only from Eastern Ontario?" Obviously, with more resources and time, an analogous volume, with hundreds of similar stories, could have been written. One finds people like this throughout the UGCC in North America – though I would not include among them the Lefevrites or other "traditionalists" who seek out Ukrainian parishes primarily for a "valid Mass." In any case, on a small budget, the only feasible way to proceed was to work with a limited group of people living in the same vicinity.

As for other reasons that I believed a book like this was crucial: for decades, a fair number of us cradle Ukrainian Catholics have been frustrated – nay, depressed – about the refusal of the UGCC in Western countries to become the Church that Patriarch Sviatoslav[2] and his Church of the martyrs call us to be.[3] To be vibrant, the Ukrainian Catholic Church obviously cannot be a "Catholic Church for Ukrainians" – understood restrictively. As Sviatoslav's predecessor, Archbishop Andrey Sheptytsky, insisted, this would be ecclesiological heresy. The saintly Sheptytsky wrote: "Any Church that would duplicate national divisions and animosities would cease to be Christ's Church."[4] These words, penned in 1901, at the very beginning of his 44-year ministry as primate of the Church in present-day Western Ukraine, guided all of the Archbishop's work.

---

2   In the recent book-length interview with Patriarch Sviatoslav, entitled *Dialoh likuye rany* [Dialogue heals wounds], the Primate of the UGCC says: "Visiting our parishes in the USA [recently], I constantly repeated: 'We are a Ukrainian Church – but not just for Ukrainians. In a city in Arizona, near the Mexican border, our [UGCC] priest, describing his parish, told me – in troubled tones – that a big issue in his parish was that while many Mexicans and people of other nationalities are captivated by our Liturgy, there are few Ukrainians there. Moreover, the Ukrainians have trouble reconciling themselves to the presence of the non-Ukrainians. The priest asked me: 'What would you [Your Beatitude], advise me to do? I answered: 'I'll come to your parish and serve our Liturgy in Spanish.' And that's exactly what I did. And then I saw how all those who were there felt happy, because they sensed that they had been accepted – they felt they were at home. Consequently, to the extent that I can, I try to break down ethnic prejudice and to show that we are a Catholic Church, that is, a universal Church." *Dialoh likuye rany* (Lviv: Svichado, 2018), 157–58.

3   Archbishop Borys Gudziak of the Philadelphia Archeparchy, a Harvard PhD who moved to Ukraine in 1992 to create an Institute that, among other tasks, collected the testimony of Soviet-era Ukrainian confessors of the faith, has written: "Pope John Paul II's solemn proclamation of the new martyrs and faithful servants of God of the Ukrainian Greek Catholic Church as blessed [beatified] is another divine manifestation to our people. During more than 1000 years of salvation history on our land, Ukrainian Christians have rejoiced in various signs of God's presence … Will we be able here and now, and then tomorrow and at other times, to respond to this appearance of the Lord? Are we ready to witness to Christ in everyday life or, God forbid, if the need arises, in the face of mortal danger? We hope in the Lord that this is so." Borys Gudziak, "Holiness in Life," in Oleh Turij, ed., *Church of the Martyrs: The New Saints of Ukraine* (Lviv: Institute of Church History and Catechetical-Pedagogical Institute of the Ukrainian Catholic University, 2004), 3, 5.

4   *"Pravdyva vira"* [The true faith], in Anatol Bazylewycz, ed., *Works of the Servant of God Metropolitan Andrei Sheptytsky – Pastoral Letters* (Toronto: Basilian Press, 1965), 66. See also *"Pravdy viry"* [The truths of the faith], ibid., 38.

Among Eastern Christians, whether Catholic or Orthodox, this key tenet of Christian ecclesiology is frequently forgotten. But the reasons are not surprising – if nonetheless unacceptable: for centuries, many Eastern Churches have been compelled by a brutal history to become chaplains, as it were, to defenceless ethnic and national groups. Seeing their political leadership decimated, their language proscribed and their culture mocked, Ukrainians, for example, turned to the Church as a surrogate state. The Church can only be proud that a nation being raped psychologically – and physically – turned to her for solace. But as Sheptytsky always insisted, there are temporal solutions and eternal ones, and the eternal ones (called salvation) should never be supplanted by the temporal. It is only the eternal that will *ultimately* help a nation deal with its woes. Sheptytsky's patriotism – rather than nationalism – compelled him to provide Ukrainians with what he knew was the best: a sincere and effective belief in the living God.[5] The nine non-Ukrainians described here are spiritual children of Sheptytsky. More specifically, they have been smitten by Sheptytsky's stress on liturgical prayer permeated by a genuine Eastern Christian lifestyle.

As for the question of proselytism, Protestants reading this book will be happy to know that I have sometimes discouraged seekers – including some described in this book – from joining the UGCC. First, I strongly believe in "not preaching the gospel, where Christ has already been named, lest I build on someone else's foundation" (Romans 15:20). Second, I was afraid that they could end up losing what they had gained in their former religious communities (such

---

5   Certainly, only an awareness of the eternal could motivate Sheptytsky to risk his own life, not to mention the lives of his clergy and nuns, by sheltering more than 150 Jews during the Holocaust. The remarkable nature of the Archbishop's faithful courage has been described thus: "No other ecclesiastical figure of equal rank in the whole of Europe displayed such sorrow for the fate of the Jews and acted so boldly on their behalf." Eric Goldhagen, Lecturer in Jewish Studies, Harvard University, in the Introduction to David Kahane, *Lvov Ghetto Diary* (Amherst, MA: University of Massachusetts Press, 1990). Kahane was sheltered by Sheptytsky. For information on the acknowledgement of Sheptytsky's heroism, see Peter Galadza, ed., *Archbishop Andrey Sheptytsky and the Ukrainian Jewish Bond* (Ottawa: Ukrainian Jewish Encounter and Sheptytsky Institute, 2014).

is the state of some of our UGCC parishes). And third, today there is the problem of "church shopping – and hopping." Consumerism affects even religion.

Regarding the first fear, these people sought our Church. We didn't seek them. Certainly, if the UGCC should be seeking anyone it should be its own cradle members who, for various reasons, have left her to become agnostics, or worse. Moreover, millions of other people in North America have never known the power and healing of Christ's Gospel. It is these that should be the focus of any Church. But God has given the UGCC these blessed seekers, and we would be foolish to reject the gift.

This leads to the response to the second fear. After a while, it became apparent that these newcomers had been sent by God (if I may speak so assuredly of divine activity) not primarily to profit from what our Church has to offer, but to benefit us – to confirm us in our faith.

Consequently, the real risk that they could lose their knowledge of scripture, see their apostolic zeal wane and diminish their involvement in humanitarian service seemed to be outweighed by the risk that not having them in the UGCC would deprive the latter of a desperately needed "leaven" (see Matthew 13:33).

As for the third and final concern, none of the individuals described here ever displayed the signs of "Church shopping." Others have, but not these nine. Quite the contrary. This makes their ability to commit in an age of fluidity all the more inspiring.[6] Of course, the cynic will respond that it may only be a matter of time before they move on. But one could respond – with equal cynicism – that so many cradle Ukrainian Catholics leave their Church every year that almost any kind of effort at revival

---

6 A fascinating presentation on commitment – and much more – by Harold and Rebecca Visse can be viewed at https://youtu.be/dTWtprKOnBs. "Parents, Children and the Challenges of Secularism," presented at "Relationships in an Age of Fluidity," the annual MASI Study Days, organized by the Sheptytsky Institute, University of St. Michael's College, University of Toronto, July 5, 2015. The video includes references to a facet of their lives not narrated in the present chapter – their work as "soccer parents."

is futile. However, cynics are called to stand with Ezekiel and watch new life rise from dry bones (see Ezekiel 37:1-14).

Incidentally, I must note that we cradle UGCC members will be guilty of a contemptuous ploy if we look upon such newcomers primarily as donors who can keep our parishes afloat during a time of declining membership and dwindling finances. No one likes to be used, and "users" should be exposed. Occasionally, UGCC talk of evangelization derives from precisely such financial considerations. Presumably, this would mean that if we could again fill our pews with "real" Ukrainians, we wouldn't need "the others." We all know how authentic Christianity is damaged by such institutional reasoning. However, I must add that, surprisingly, the UGCC sometimes displays a better record of hospitality than other "ethnic Churches." I say "surprisingly" because the same nation that has been wounded owing to a lack of strong geographical and other boundaries has also allowed those porous frontiers to serve, on occasion, as cordial channels into the community. Among Ukrainians, the experience of suffering has sometimes inspired unexpected affection toward the marginalized.

In a similar vein regarding "institutional reasoning," this very book will be guilty of such self-promotion if it is used by Ukrainian Catholics as a vanity publication – showcasing an ethnic community and "its Church." As Saint Paul proclaims, "Far be it from me to boast except in the cross of our Lord Jesus Christ, by which the world has been crucified to me and I to the world" (Galatians 6:14). Any other approach risks idolatry.

I hinted above how these "converts" helped convert me – especially from despair. By the late 1990s, I was beginning to wonder whether the Eastern tradition, which I had spent a lifetime strenuously promoting, stood a chance of survival in Western countries. That tradition, when practised authentically, is so counter-cultural! It is ascetical, musically demanding and challenging in its liturgical ethos. By that I mean that in the Eastern rites, keeping the average worshipper interested is harder. That's because (fortunately) the worshipper is far less the focus of attention than the Worshipped. (My apologies for not being able to explain here what may be interpreted as a rather pretentious claim.) In any case, just as I was losing heart, God put me in touch with – or drew me closer to – the people described here. Even more importantly, these people fed the faith of our children. For my wife Olenka and me, these newcomers were a Godsend: our children got to know them during their teenage years, when young people frequently leave the faith. Their witness provided much-needed credibility.

Many cradle Eastern Christians who feel that their traditional ascetical and liturgical practices are simply unrealistic will read these accounts and cry "romanticism" – or worse. So the question arises: How is it that the classical Byzantine Christian lifestyle, viewed as impractical by those raised in this tradition, appeals to these newcomers? There is an adage that helps explain the anomaly: "Rules without a relationship breed rebellion." Certainly "the narrow gate" (see Matthew 7:13) of historic Eastern Christianity will spawn resentment if a loving bond with the living God is absent. Few people enjoy performing acts of affection for someone they're not in love with. This is the key. All of these "converts," or "switchers," described here fell in love with Christ in their original Christian communities and "switched" only because they experienced a UGCC community where the acts of affection could be performed in a way that seemed to express that relationship more fully.

This is the point at which the question of Eastern triumphalism should be addressed. No doubt, for every publication about Western Christians "going East," one could theoretically write several tomes about justified movement in the opposite direction. Consequently, in spite of the oblique – and not so oblique – criticism of Western Christian traditions occasionally found in the interviews transcribed here, the credit for doing the important work of inoculating the nine interviewees from rebellion goes to their Protestant and Roman Catholic parents. It is these Western Christians who nurtured the relationship with Christ that their children brought with them into the UGCC. No wonder, then, that in all of the cases recounted here, not a single parent begrudged their child's journey to their new community. In fact, if memory serves me right, the Protestant parents were always present at their children's reception into the Ukrainian Catholic Church. I presume they were proud that they had raised such good missionaries. In any case, the Ukrainian Greco-Catholic Church theoretically has the potential to meld the best of Eastern Christianity with the best of its Western counterpart. And even if sometimes it has instead melded the worst aspects of both, this book is about potential – not problems.

A note about the prominence of liturgy in the narratives recounted here may also be necessary. Hopefully, the interviews that Chris Guly has masterfully transcribed dispel any suspicions of liturgical reductionism. The nine newcomers obviously possess an approach to worship that is holistic. It's not about "smells and bells." Romans 12:1, with its reference to what constitutes "rational" worship, guides them, as it should. The Pauline scriptural phrase – "rational," "spiritual" or even "comprehensive" worship – is how the Byzantine liturgical tradition describes itself. In other words, if one asks a Greco-Catholic or Eastern Orthodox what they are doing in church, they should quote their own liturgical texts (see the Eucharistic Prayers of Chrysostom and Basil the Great) and respond that they are engaging in a form of adoration and service that engulfs the totality of one's life and being.

Bishop Robert Barron, the brilliant Catholic evangelist, stresses the importance of beauty in attracting people to Christ – and keeping them attracted. Good Eastern liturgy is certainly beautiful, and it is the evening services of the Ukrainian Church that come up again and again in the interviews offered here. St. John the Baptist parish in Ottawa has indeed become a shrine that all of us carry in our hearts wherever we go. And the laypeople there, who have kept those services going at times even without clergy, testify not only to the power of divine beauty, but to the power of the laity as well.

May every Church in Canada be blessed with such "strange" people. Or, to re-deploy a term used by Stanley Hauerwas and

William Willimon,[7] may our world be increasingly populated by such "aliens."[8]

Peter Galadza

*Sheptytsky Institute
of Eastern Christian Studies*

*University of St. Michael's College
in the University of Toronto*

---

7   *Resident Aliens: Life in the Christian Colony* (Nashville, TN: Abingdon Press, 1989).

8   For more theological reflection on this issue, see Peter Galadza, "Multiple Belongings and Transnational Processes of Catholic Formation in an Eastern Catholic Church," in Michael L. Budde, ed., *Beyond the Borders of Baptism: Catholicity, Allegiances, and Lived Identities* (Eugene, OR: Wipf and Stock, 2016), 123–40; and Peter Galadza, "The Structure of the Eastern Churches: Bonded with Human Blood or Baptismal Water?" *Pro Ecclesia* 17 (2008): 373–86.

1

Harold and Rebecca Visser: Two Magnets Attracting Others

Harold and Rebecca speaking at the annual
Sheptytsky Institute Study Days about Commitment.

The Vissers' own "soccer team."

Attend the English-language Divine Liturgy at Ottawa's St. John the Baptist Ukrainian Catholic Shrine on any given Sunday and chances are you will meet – or be greeted by – Harold and Rebecca Visser.

Arguably, this unlikeliest of couples has helped fill the pews with new and long-standing Ukrainian Catholics eager to worship in a vibrant Byzantine liturgy accented by young melodic singers and clear and crisp readings. The Vissers have also ensured that the welcome mat extends, after the Mass has ended, into the church hall, where parishioners and visitors have the opportunity to socialize over hot soup or chili and pastries well into the afternoon.

Hospitality comes naturally for Harold and Rebecca, an outgoing and take-charge couple who have been married since October 1997. But the setting for such warmth is more a reflection of adult choice than childhood background. Neither of the Vissers is of Ukrainian descent, nor were either raised in a Catholic family. But love and circumstance brought them to the Ukrainian Catholic Church, which for them has become a place for both spiritual and community enrichment.

Harold was born in Vancouver in 1973 to parents raised in the Dutch Reformed tradition in their native Netherlands. "They both had fallen from their faith, and when they came from Holland separately in the late 1960s, they met in Vancouver as part of the hippie scene," says Harold. "My dad, and then my mom, underwent a major Christian conversion and I was only born because of that. They had not planned on having kids, and ended up having seven!"

Allan, his father, who pursued a career in education, and Nanne, his mother, who left nursing to raise the seven children, belonged to a non-denominational charismatic congregation; their "awareness of God never left me throughout my life," says Harold.

Self-identifying as an Evangelical Christian, he entered Trinity Western University in Langley, British Columbia, on a scholarship, where he pursued biblical studies and was active on campus. Harold served as managing editor of the student newspaper and created a syllabus for a practicum course in communications. He also sang in the university's chamber choir and played on the varsity soccer team. But a unique initiative caught Harold's attention and took him in an entirely new direction.

In 1994, the Challenge Team, a non-profit organization that promoted healthy sexuality among young people, was about to embark on a second cross-country "chastity" tour. Harold, an ardent pro-lifer, jumped on board expecting to only talk about abstinence to teens across Canada. He didn't know the Challenge Team would lead him to a wife and a new life in Ottawa. As it turned out, Rebecca, who had completed an undergraduate degree in political science and history at the University of Alberta, was one of the organizers of the tour.

Born in Edmonton in 1971, Rebecca had a different backstory than Harold. Her father, Fawzy Morcos, was born in Egypt and met her Dutch-born mother, Corry, in England; Corry worked as a midwife at the hospital where Fawzy completed his medical studies to become an obstetrician and gynecologist. The couple was married in the Church of England and immigrated to Canada in 1969, settling in Edmonton. Rebecca, their firstborn of four children, was baptized in the Coptic Orthodox Church, according to her father's faith tradition. "But we were raised in the Anglican Church, where my parents felt most at home," explains Rebecca.

The Morcoses worshipped at an Evangelical Anglican church in Edmonton, and Rebecca attended Roman Catholic schools. "Unlike Harold, I was exposed to the Catholic faith when I was growing up, and my best friends were Catholic," she says. That contact gradually changed Rebecca's view of religion. "I had been raised with a very narrow definition of what it meant to be a Christian: that you could only be a Christian if you were born again, say the Sinner's Prayer, and invite Jesus into your heart," she explains. "By university, I started to question what salvation means and what it really means to be a Christian."

Rebecca organized a pro-life group at the U of A, through which she met "amazingly faithful Catholics" who inspired her to think beyond her familiar faith – and to come up with the idea of the speaking tour. The aim of the tour, as she explains, was to "prevent abortion by helping young women to not get pregnant in the first place."

In 1993, a group of 11 Challenge Team volunteer members assembled in Montreal and drove to Vancouver in a 15-passenger rental van, stopping along the way to bring their message about abstaining from pre-marital sex to schools and church youth groups. Costs were kept to a minimum. Speakers stayed in homes of supporters and relied on home-cooked meals. Revenue was also at a minimum; each presentation only garnered the group between $100 and $150 – enough to cover the cost of vehicle rental, but not much else. In the same year, Rebecca moved to Ottawa to begin an internship with Focus on the Family. Based on the first tour's success reaching 13,000 students, she decided to organize another one in 1994 – and this time, Harold was involved.

The second tour was divided into two groups of 24 speakers squeezed into two vans: one headed east from Ottawa to Newfoundland, and the other travelled west. Harold was with the latter group, which moved at an exhausting clip from Ottawa to Edmonton to Victoria back to Ottawa in six weeks from the end of April to the middle of June 1994. During that short period, both teams made about 400 presentations. Based on the positive feedback the Challenge Team received, Rebecca, Harold and two other members decided that an annual tour had the potential to become a permanent initiative.

Harold relocated to Ottawa and became administrator of the Challenge Team, whose office was in the basement of a house on Main Street, not far from Saint Paul University, where the Metropolitan Andrey Sheptytsky Institute of Eastern Christian Studies was then situated. The location proved important for Harold, who by then had become familiar with Catholicism through the Catholics who participated in the national speaking tour.

"That was my first real engagement with Catholics," he explains. "We had great discussions about faith, and I came off that six-week tour thinking I was probably going to become a Catholic."

"I wasn't so much rejecting my Evangelical heritage, but I recognized that it lacked a more fulsome theology, a Eucharistic life and a social ethic that the Catholic Church has. Being an Evangelical Christian was not enough for me."

Rebecca, who was just a friend and colleague to Harold at the time, had already made her decision and joined the Roman Catholic Church in 1995. It took Harold a couple of years to arrive at the same point. He had begun reading about Eastern Christianity, and for a time considered joining an Orthodox congregation.

But the Sheptytsky Institute was just down the street from the Challenge Team office, and Harold heard about regular prayer services held at the chapel. He decided to attend, liked what he saw, had lively conversations with the Institute's liturgy professor, Fr. Peter Galadza, and became a regular worshipper.

All of this led Harold to make what would become a life-changing decision. "It became clear to me that it was important that I be a Catholic, but I had developed enough of an appreciation of Eastern spirituality that it had to be something other than Roman Catholicism," he explains.

The Ukrainian Catholic Church seemed to him the logical destination for his spiritual journey. St. John the Baptist was and remains the only Ukrainian Catholic parish in Ottawa – and it offered an English-language liturgy, a bonus for Harold, who is fluent in Dutch but understood not a word of Ukrainian at the time.

He began preparing to join the Church and arranged for a full-immersion baptism at the shrine during the Paschal Vigil on March 29, 1997. The trouble was the church didn't have a baptismal font big enough to accommodate a grown man. So Harold improvised. He and some friends obtained a large recycling bin, about 1.5 metres high and less than a metre wide, from Saint Paul University. Fortunately, it was on wheels, so transporting the thing was made a lot easier.

He also ensured that friends and parishioners present for the baptism didn't witness him being dunked in what was effectively a large garbage can. The bin, draped in white cloth covered in

Ukrainian embroidery and filled with water, became a baptismal font.

At the time, Harold and Rebecca were good friends, and in fact went from Harold's baptism at St. John the Baptist to the Easter Vigil at St. Mary's Roman Catholic Church, which Rebecca attended. "Our first date was a couple of weeks after my baptism," recalls Harold. "And we were married that October." Nine months later, Rebecca gave birth to the couple's first of seven children (five sons and two daughters) born between 1998 and 2012.

When she was pregnant with their fourth child in 2002, they also decided to close the Challenge Team office, particularly after the group lost a Federal Court challenge to obtain charitable status two years earlier.

The Vissers' focus changed. While Rebecca concentrated on raising their growing family, Harold returned to school – in a major way. He received his bachelor's degree in theology from Saint Paul University in 2005, focusing on Eastern Christian studies, and followed it with a Master of Arts, also in Eastern Christian theology, from the same university in 2011. His thesis was on prayer in the home. For Harold, it was as practical a research project as it was academic, since he and Rebecca raised their children – all baptized Ukrainian Catholics – with the objective of living their faith beyond their time in church.

On a more career-oriented stream, Harold also obtained a master's degree in pastoral theology from Saint Paul University in 2016, with a research focus on high school chaplaincy. It provided him with the academic background and practical training to serve as a chaplain in a Catholic secondary school in the Ottawa area. By then, Harold and Rebecca had decided which church would become home base.

But it had not always been thus. Before they got married, Rebecca was still attached to St. Mary's, a Roman Catholic parish run by the Companions of the Cross, a conservative community of priests based in Ottawa. Harold's heart was with St. John the Baptist, so the couple decided to attend each church on alternate

Sundays. "All of our friends were at St. Mary's," explains Rebecca. "There were very few young adults and young married couples at St. John the Baptist, so it was difficult to choose."

In 1998, they settled on the Shrine, which offered both of them the right blend of Catholic teaching and Eastern Christian spirituality. But in so doing, the Vissers became pioneers as much as parishioners at the church. "We were the only couple there where neither one of us was Ukrainian," says Rebecca. "But we're both first-born in our families, and we both like to take the initiative and feel comfortable stepping in and trying to move things along."

At the noon-hour English-language Divine Liturgy, Harold and Rebecca – as part of a small choir – would only recite the propers, as they hadn't yet learned how to sing them. That would come, since both of them were partly drawn to Ukrainian Catholicism because of the liturgical music. In any case, the Vissers decided that they and their children would be active worshippers at the liturgy, loudly singing hymns and reciting prayers.

Initially, they were seen as "interlopers," recalls Rebecca. "Some parishioners couldn't understand why we were in a Ukrainian Catholic church when we're not Ukrainian. It was unfathomable to them." Harold remembers one particular conversation. "I was asked, 'Is your mom Ukrainian?' I said no. 'Your grandparents?' No. There was an assumption that there had to be a biological reason for being in this church."

It was faith and not culture that brought the Vissers to St. John the Baptist, explains Rebecca, who is technically a Coptic Catholic, since she didn't formally change rites when she joined the Catholic Church. "We're first and foremost Catholics. We attend a Ukrainian Catholic church because of its beautiful expression of faith and the richness of its liturgical life. It also helps that there are liturgies and other services in English, because I don't understand Ukrainian." (Harold can read Cyrillic and speak a few Ukrainian words.)

But the Vissers wouldn't remain oddities for long. Other young, non-Ukrainian families joined the church, including the Butchers (see chapter 2), who helped enliven the English liturgy with a choir

21

steeped in the Byzantine musical tradition. Students from the Sheptytsky Institute and Holy Spirit Ukrainian Catholic Seminary (which have since relocated to Toronto and Edmonton respectively) also began attending the Sunday morning Liturgy.

What's most striking today is that of the 100 to 150 people who attend the Divine Liturgy, many are not of Ukrainian descent. Some weren't born Catholic; more were Roman Catholics. All of them were looking for a "traditional worship environment that is both joyful and sacred," explains Harold, who has served as the liturgical coordinator at St. John the Baptist since 2005.

But this spiritual appetite extends beyond Sundays.

Saturday evening English-language vespers – a rarity in Ukrainian Catholic churches across Canada – has also become a must-attend for many non-Ukrainians at St. John the Baptist. Harold occasionally serves as cantor, always prepares the propers for the service and at one time would arrange for a Ukrainian Catholic priest – the late Fr. Bob Anderson – to deliver 90-minute lectures on topics of faith before the 6 p.m. vespers. This began as part of a monthly series called "Light and Life."

Vespers are also held on weekdays on the eves of feasts. When no priest is available to lead the service, the congregation runs it. And a new addition – matins held before the Sunday English liturgy – is entirely lay-led.

To complement Sunday morning catechism, the Vissers organized a children's homily during the English liturgy's regular sermon, when young parishioners head downstairs to the parish hall (or outside, on warm days) to discuss the gospel of the day.

Not only do the Vissers give of their time and talents, they have also helped provide resources for the Shrine – from buying liturgical anthologies for worship to purchasing a baptismal font for the church. "It's our tithe and no different than those who put money into things that are important to them," says Harold. It's a reflection of the Vissers' commitment to St. John the Baptist, which they view as both a house of worship and a place for community.

As Harold explains: "To have a healthy parish, you need to have three pillars: good liturgy, good teaching and good fellowship. You need all three to survive and thrive." The fellowship component is also partly a Visser gift to the English-speaking congregation at St. John the Baptist. Rather than having people rush home for lunch after the liturgy, the couple, along with a few other families, thought it would be better to gather together empty stomachs in the parish hall as an opportunity to socialize and get to know one another better.

The Vissers usually provide some doughnuts, and they and other families take turns bringing soup or chili and bread to the post-liturgy luncheon. Sometimes, the menu goes exotic with curry (provided by Brian Butcher, who is of Indian descent) or vegan, courtesy of a group of university students. Others bring cakes and cookies. (A scaled-down reception of soup and bread is also provided after the Lenten Liturgy of the Presanctified Gifts and other services throughout the year.) The teen parishioners handle clean-up after the lunch. "The idea is to create a sense that the church is a community and not a place where you walk in, attend a service and walk out," explains Harold. "The Church is not a fast-food restaurant where you get the stuff you need and leave. It's supposed to be a gourmet meal with others where you take the time to be present and share, and have all your senses – seeing, hearing, smelling – touched, and not just your taste buds."

He says that neither he nor Rebecca have ever had any pushback from any of their seven children not wanting to attend church as a family. "Some may not be that into the teaching aspect or the fellowship, but it's enough of an experience for them that they all want to be there," says Harold.

"Each of our kids realize that it enhances their life and makes it something beautiful, and that they can only achieve that if they go in deep enough to experience all aspects of life at St. John the Baptist." As he adds: "You undercut yourself if you only strive for the minimum requirement of attending church on Sundays and leaving when the liturgy ends. You can only develop a sense of belonging by praying together, learning together and sharing fellowship together."

But perhaps the best example of the extended spiritual family the Vissers helped create at St. John's is one of heartbreaking tragedy. When Rebecca was pregnant in late 2009, the couple informed their friends at the parish that ultrasounds detected that their unborn baby had both a congenital diaphragmatic hernia (a potentially life-threatening fetal abnormality in which the diaphragm muscle that separates the chest from the abdomen fails to close during prenatal development, and the contents from the abdomen move into the chest and leave little room for the lungs to grow) and Trisomy 18, a genetic disorder caused by the presence of all or some of a third copy of chromosome 18.

The Vissers' worst fears were realized when their daughter, Lily Emke, died when Rebecca went into labour shortly after midnight on February 21, 2010. "It happened at a time in our lives when it was still somewhere on our radar to consider moving back to the West to be closer to our families," Rebecca now recalls. "But the way the church community gathered around us to support us affirmed how deep our roots were in Ottawa." Hundreds of people attended a poignant open-casket funeral for Lily, held at the Shrine on February 25, 2010. "The service itself was intensely healing for me," says Rebecca, who with Harold, memorialized their daughter in a blog (https://lilyemkevisser.blogspot.com).

"Harold had researched the liturgical text specifically for the funeral and burial of an infant in the Byzantine tradition, and the prayers and music gave me so much peace on an extremely difficult day."

"We had been married in the Ukrainian Catholic Church – the first wedding either of us had attended in the Church – had baptized our six children up to that point in the Church, and had experienced the richness and thoughtfulness of the Church's funeral rite. This was now our home."

2

Brian Butcher: In Search of a Spiritual Identity

Brian Butcher at the American Academy of Religion with a prepublication copy of his book, *Liturgical Theology after Schmemann*.

Brian Butcher warms up the Sheptytsky Institute Choir before a performance at the Ottawa Ukrainian Festival.

At both the professional and personal levels, Brian Butcher has been both intrigued and driven by the notion of identity. His doctoral thesis in theology, recently published as a monograph by Fordham University Press (*Liturgical Theology after Schmemann: An Orthodox Reading of Paul Ricoeur*, 2018) focused on the work of a 20th-century French philosopher who wrote extensively about the formation of identity – how symbols, metaphors and narratives help provide an understanding of the self and how literature explores the recognition of "otherness." Finding a spiritual identity, however, involved a much longer process of self-discovery for Butcher, who often found himself feeling like an "other."

Twelve days after he was born in Winnipeg in 1975, Butcher was adopted by a missionary Baptist couple, the Rev. Colin and the late Merle Butcher. His birth parents were a young, unmarried couple who were unable to look after him. Butcher's late biological father, Carm Mascarenhas, whom he never met, was a musician from the heavily Catholic Indian state of Goa, who came to Canada and settled in Winnipeg in the hope of finding a place in the city's bustling jazz scene. Butcher's mother, Mary Lebrun, an American who lives in Arizona and is of French and Belgian ancestry, had roots in the farming communities of North Dakota. Her father had moved the family to Winnipeg, where he had a highly successful career as professor of history at the University of Manitoba.

Perhaps Butcher inherited his academic genes from the Lebruns and his musical DNA (he also plays piano and guitar, and sings) from the Mascarenhas clan (although, as he points out, the Lebruns are also very gifted musically). But it was the Butchers who helped put him on a path to finding out where he came from and where he was headed in life.

At the age of 10, Butcher moved from Winnipeg with his adoptive parents and younger brother to Pakistan, where the Baptist couple, who had spent nine years in India, began their second round of missionary work. (His family also included an older sister – born to the Butchers – as well as an older brother adopted from the northern Indian state of Assam.) "That's where I gained a lively sense of my Indian heritage, inasmuch as Pakistan used to be part of India," explains Butcher, who thought he would become a Baptist missionary like his parents.

But as a teen, he found himself fascinated by religious symbols that were distinctly non-Protestant. "Even as an Evangelical, beauty and mystery were important to me. In my quiet prayer time, I would dim the lights in my room, burn a candle, light a stick of incense, and sit cross-legged on the floor in the lotus position and read the Bible. I had picked up enough from the New Age influences I encountered in high school that I felt it important to set the stage for my encounter with God. My dad would laugh and say, 'There's our little Hindu.'"

"I realized later that I was meant to connect further with my Indian heritage, and as I grew older, I cultivated an interest in all things Indian. In 2015, I finally went to India, spending two months in Kerala with the Syro-Malankara, one of the several 'Thomas Christian' communities. Although my father was deceased at the time, I also went to Goa and met my birth family – his siblings and my cousins," recalls Butcher, who, at the age of 25, had already made contact with his biological mother and his maternal relatives.

By then, he was married with two children. He met their mother, who was of Korean descent, at McGill University in Montreal, from which he graduated in 1998 with a B.A. in Religious and Middle East Studies, and a minor in East Asian Studies. As Butcher had begun to discover his ethnic roots, he had also, by then, found his spiritual family.

Although raised as an Evangelical, and married in the Anglican Church, Butcher attended and provided music ministry at the Newman Centre, the Roman Catholic chaplaincy at McGill, named after the famed 19th-century English theologian John Henry Newman, an Anglican priest who converted to Catholicism and was made a cardinal by Pope Leo XIII. "But I had fallen in love with the Christian East after visiting an English-speaking Orthodox church in Montreal," explains Butcher. "I would often go there for vespers and was reading my way through Orthodox theology."

He found himself in a quandary: how could he embrace both Orthodoxy, which he loved for its mystical and liturgical traditions, and Catholicism, to which he was attracted because of, in his view, the clarity of its moral teaching? The answer came to him when he attended a presentation by staff from Madonna House, a Catholic apostolate for priests and laity in Combermere, Ontario. Madonna House had been founded by the late Catherine (Kolyschkine) Doherty, who was born into a devout Russian Orthodox family in the late 19th century, joined the Roman Catholic Church in the early 20th century, and spent the rest of her life promoting the merits of both faith traditions.

Butcher was inspired by Doherty's writings that espoused what Pope Saint John Paul II would later describe as the Church breathing with its two (Eastern and Western) lungs. "I remember, when my first daughter [Jasmine] was born, sitting in a rocking chair and reading in one all-night sitting Catherine's autobiography, *Fragments of My Life*," recalls Butcher. "How beautiful it was that this woman, who grew up in Russia, felt equally at home in the Latin rite as in the Byzantine rite, seeing them as complementary expressions of the same faith."

Butcher pursued that vision until it led him to the Ukrainian Catholic Church, into which he was chrismated in Montreal on November 21, 1998 – the feast of the Entrance of the Mother of God into the Temple.

Inquisitive by nature, he wanted to know more about his new faith, especially its liturgical traditions; he was directed by Fr. Roman Lahola (the Montreal priest who had received him into full communion) to seek the counsel of Fr. Peter Galadza at the Sheptytsky Institute of Eastern Christian Studies.

"I met Fr. Peter, and he dropped what he was doing and gave me three hours of his time. Over coffee I peppered him with question after question, for each of which he had a sound answer. By the end of it I was satisfied that this was the Church I was meant to join," says Butcher, who ultimately found his mentor in Galadza.

"At the end of our conversation, he said to me, 'You know, Brian, if at the end of the day you use us as a stepping stone to Orthodoxy, that's okay.' And I said to myself, what kind of a guy is so at peace, so confident in his own identity, that he can actually say 'you can use us' if God is calling you somewhere else and you need to come *through* us to go there. He recognizes that he doesn't have a monopoly on truth or on God's providence – and I thought, that's the Church I want to belong to!"

But living in Montreal at the time, Butcher had no regular opportunity to worship in a Ukrainian Catholic church, so he would pray the Liturgy of the Hours at home while continuing his involvement with the Newman Centre.

After spending a year in South Korea studying Korean, Butcher moved to Ottawa in 2000 and began to attend St. John the Baptist Ukrainian Catholic Shrine, along with occasional visits to the Melkite parish of Sts. Peter and Paul. A year later, intending to become a priest, he entered Holy Spirit Ukrainian Catholic Seminary, then in Ottawa.

"It was a challenging time because we had just had our third child, and my wife felt our family to be overwhelmed by the intensity of the seminary formation, which does demand a lot from the candidates," explains Butcher. "Although married students were allowed, the seminary's schedule was originally designed for celibate candidates in terms of the hours one was expected to keep. You had to be present at 6:30 a.m. liturgies, and build your life around that, so it was difficult logistically for us."

"There was also a strong ethno-cultural atmosphere, with Ukrainian used as the exclusive language of worship every second week. Unfortunately, I didn't understand Ukrainian at the time, and my own family's ethnicity and culture were, of course, rather different. But I loved our chant in any language – how it spoke to my soul!"

At the time, Butcher was also pursuing graduate studies in theology at the Sheptytsky Institute, and felt somewhat disconnected from the other seminarians, who were predominantly in undergraduate programs. After a year, Butcher set aside his seminary formation to focus on his studies, proceeding to complete his M.A. thesis in 2003: "Convoluted Conjugality: Hymnographic Repression, Transference and Co-optation in the Byzantine Sanctoral's Commemoration of Married Saints." His research examined how married saints had historically been marginalized in liturgical texts. It was as much a reflection of his own feelings of being on the periphery in his faith journey as it was an academic exploration of the Byzantine tradition's representation of non-celibate holy people.

After joining St. John the Baptist, Butcher felt a deep connection to the parish community, even when he packed up his family in 2006 (now with six children) and moved to British Columbia, where he would spend five years finishing his doctoral dissertation, and teaching theology and religious studies at several institutions, including The Seminary of Christ the King, Corpus Christi College at the University of British Columbia, as well as Trinity Western and Simon Fraser Universities. "But our heart was really in Ottawa, especially with our friends at St. John the Baptist, which is such a special group of people," he says.

Not surprisingly, Butcher jumped at the chance to return to the national capital in 2011 when an opportunity arose at the Sheptytsky Institute to fill in for Galadza, who was about to go on sabbatical. When Galadza returned, Butcher was asked to remain, and has since served in various capacities.

He has also become a highly active parishioner at St. John the Baptist Shrine, participating in the development of a dynamic English-speaking community, more than half of whom, like him, have no Ukrainian roots, but have solidified within the parish a vibrant liturgical and social life.

Some of that vigour is the result of the church's location, says Butcher. "For decades, the combined influence of the Seminary and Institute served to attract a greater proportion of non-Ukrainians to our church than perhaps any other parish in the country."

It has also resulted in the introduction to the church of many more liturgical services conducted in English, including the Divine

Liturgy of the Presanctified Gifts during Lent, Saturday evening and festal vespers, Sunday morning matins and the Penitential Canon of St. Andrew of Crete – as well as a full slate of Holy Week offerings. All of this has "cultivated a sense of living the feasts and the fasts, the seasons of the Church year," Butcher explains. "It's about trying to cull all the spiritual riches available to us in the Byzantine tradition, which even many Orthodox churches in the West are prone to neglect. Many parishioners of Ukrainian descent, perhaps surprisingly, have come to (re)discover their own tradition as experienced through the eyes, ears and zeal of those who have come in from the outside."

He admits that the Sheptytsky Institute's move to Toronto in 2017 and the Seminary's relocation to Edmonton in 2018 have generated apprehension within the Anglophone community at St. John the Baptist as to whether the "infusion of new blood" hitherto effected by both institutions might cease. "We're intent on that *not* happening," insists Butcher. "It's a new era for our community, I think: a time to come into its own. We've been given so much, but now we have to stand on our own two feet because we no longer have those external supports."

He suggests that whereas other Canadian Ukrainian Catholic churches with a similarly broad liturgical schedule and sense of outreach might well depend upon strong clerical vision and leadership, St. John the Baptist has especially benefited from lay initiatives: many families take turns, for example, cooking meals for the entire community following the Sunday Divine Liturgy. And something as important as cantoring is the shared responsibility of many adults and, importantly, children and youth.

"We've seen something of a snowball effect over the years. The more things there are available, the more people want to come out. It's not just a church to visit to satisfy one's Sunday 'obligation,' but a community in which people see each other several times a week at different services, forming lasting Christian friendships with one another."

Intimate rites, such as the celebration of Forgiveness Vespers at the beginning of Lent – or the mutual exchange of the Paschal kiss throughout Eastertide – "invite people to become vulnerable to a shared memory that is precious and transformative, which in turn strengthens interpersonal bonds and serves as a motivation to return year after year – to repeat, or rather reconstitute, the sacred experience anew," explains Butcher.

He adds that the often contentious matter of liturgical language represents an important pastoral orientation. "Those with no Ukrainian connection can come to the church on any Sunday and attend a Divine Liturgy that is almost entirely in English. The church has a big enough tent that you don't have to be Ukrainian to come inside – even though those of Ukrainian background find themselves entirely at home. For someone who is non-Ukrainian to say, 'I'm a Ukrainian Catholic,' however, can – and often does – elicit puzzlement. The fact that it is called 'Ukrainian Catholic Church' implies a very specific constituency. In turn, it can often prove quite a challenge for people to pass from occasional visits to regular attendance. And much more so, to naming and claiming this identity for themselves and for their children, in the belief that our parish can be a place where they can be fully themselves – whatever their cultural background might be – while also being Ukrainian Greco-Catholics in good standing."

"Sacramental belonging doesn't necessarily equal 'fitting in'. Although we speak a lot about multiculturalism in Canada, it seems to me that it is not readily apparent how a community like ours can be both cosmopolitan while also honouring its Ukrainian roots. We are a work in progress. I think there have been some growing pains in the parish as the original Ukrainian constituency has shrunk, even as the English-language constituency has increased." Butcher estimates that about 100 people regularly attend the English-language Divine Liturgy.

"In some instances, people have shifted from attending the Ukrainian liturgy to the English one, so their children can understand the service and because they appreciate the sense of

32

fellowship and enthusiasm for the fullness of the Orthodox tradition." Butcher wonders whether this demographic development might understandably breed a certain resentment in some quarters. The Ukrainian-speaking community built the church, after all, and has a legitimate concern for its own survival.

If, as a man of colour with no ethnic Ukrainian connection, Butcher has sometimes felt the tension at an emotional level, he tends to explain it from an academic perspective as a matter of cognitive dissonance. "As a non-Ukrainian, you can sympathize with Ukrainians wanting to hold onto their culture just as much as those attending an ethnically oriented Roman Catholic church do. Nobody expects an Italian or Polish parish – which we have in Ottawa – to stop being Italian or Polish," says Butcher. "So why should anyone wish for St. John the Baptist to stop being Ukrainian?"

"But the sheer presence of non-Ukrainians in our parish introduces an element of diversity that in turn brings into question the 'natural' coherence of language, culture and religion. The Ukrainian Catholic faith *is* in fact distinguishable from the culture, and you may, of course, belong to the Church regardless of your ethnicity. Nevertheless, as is the case with other Eastern Churches, the Ukrainian Catholic Church has also served as the vehicle through which the culture, language and distinctive identity of the people of Ukraine has been protected and preserved, especially in times of persecution – such as that of the last century, under communism."

"I suspect that some people in our parish, who love it *because* it's Ukrainian, may find it hard to understand why 'strangers' like me have come in. Some of them take it as a compliment and say, 'Wow, you love what we have. We're so honoured that you want it for yourself,' while others probably feel that if someone comes here for the faith, he or she should learn to accept the culture, too. It's a very complex thing!"

Arguably, the presence of non-Ukrainian parishioners has had a singularly positive impact on life at St. John the Baptist. For instance, the Knights of Columbus St. Vladimir the Great Council

9557 has acquired most of its new members from the church's English-speaking men like Butcher, who has also been ordained a subdeacon.

"I realize, after 20 years in this Church, that it's a very peculiar vocation to become an Eastern-rite Catholic," he says. "If you were a Protestant and become a Roman Catholic, you could join a church that in many places sings the same songs you used to sing in your Protestant church, so the transition might feel fairly smooth. And if you were, instead, to become Orthodox from Protestantism, you would have the luxury of finding the "True Church," without having to directly negotiate the legacy of Reformation and post-Reformation conflicts with the Catholic Church. A convert to Orthodoxy can take pride in belonging to a 'purer,' more ancient ecclesial tradition, while continuing to regard Catholicism as suspect – albeit with a more sophisticated suspicion than before!"

"If you want to become Greco-Catholic, however, you really have to pass through three doors. First, you've got to fall in love with Byzantine liturgy and spirituality. If you don't like the formality of using prayers and hymns written centuries ago, you're likely going to be frustrated with our Church because the threshold for introducing change or variety is much smaller than it is in a Roman Catholic or Protestant setting."

"Second, if you care principally about fidelity to the Eastern Christian patrimony, then it's certainly a lot easier to join the Orthodox Church because you don't have to wrestle with all the Catholic stuff that you may have had issues with – such as Catholic teaching on contraception or divorce, for example, both of which the Orthodox allow. If you want to be intentionally Eastern Catholic, that is, you are going to have to work through Catholic faith and morals: the claims of the Petrine ministry, its teaching on beginning- and end-of-life issues, on marriage and so on. For me, there is so much goodness and truth and beauty in the Western Church that I felt I could not turn my back on it. What it teaches on sexual morality – almost uniquely, among contemporary expressions of Christianity – is, I am convinced, true; with fear and trembling, as it were, and with great love for my Orthodox brethren, I believe that the Orthodox Church is lacking in this area, having neglected, or even repudiated, its own traditional teaching."

"The third door to pass through is that of committing to a particular Eastern Catholic Church. If you just want to be a generic Catholic of the Byzantine rite, so to speak, you're going to find that you end up belonging nowhere: it is simply an aggregate designation. Anywhere you go in the world, you will have to reckon with the particular history of a given community and its inherited ethnic, linguistic and cultural dynamics – and that is probably the hardest step for converts to take."

It has been a journey for Butcher and his family to feel fully at home at St. John the Baptist. "I come to church every week and I see people who don't look like me," he explains. "My kids have also reacted differently. Some of them have come to love it – they are 'cradle' Ukrainian Catholics, and realize that, theologically speaking, this is their Church as much as anyone else's; others, however, have struggled, on account of a combination of religious and cultural factors."

"But I have also realized that if you want to be part of this community, you ultimately need to cultivate at least a passive appreciation for Ukrainian culture; at the very least, you will want to know how to sing '*Mnohaya Lita*' ('Many Years'), '*Khrystos Voskres*' ('Christ is Risen') and '*Vichnaya Pamyat*' ('Memory Eternal')!"

Providentially, Butcher – who speaks seven languages (including Korean and Ukrainian) and can read in 11 languages (including Ancient Greek and Syriac) – helped facilitate the 2017 advent of St. Mother Teresa Syro-Malabar Catholic Parish, which now regularly uses St. John the Baptist Shrine for its own Eastern-rite services while the Indo-Canadian community continues to raise funds to acquire a building.

In the future, he would love to see joint services held between the two faith communities. But in the meantime, he has promoted "otherness" linguistically at St. John the Baptist by encouraging the use of French and other languages. "We have Francophones in the parish, but even using French for something like the Lord's Prayer is a bit of a push. Some people in the parish have likely thought, 'Hold on, we're Ukrainian and we also have English, and now French – what's next?' But my answer is that we've got Arabic-speaking, Dutch-speaking, Korean-speaking and Chinese-speaking people coming to the church – and there is no reason ecclesiologically speaking that we should not be open to the use of these languages."

"Indeed, Slavonic was used until the Second Vatican Council, after which Ukrainian was introduced into the liturgy – and furthermore, for several decades after the conversion of Kyivan Rus' to Christianity in 988, Greek remained the language of the liturgy," says Butcher. "Over time, the Kyivan Rus' identity has taken on a more ethnic, national character because of the vicissitudes of history – and yet I still see the Ukrainian Catholic Church as an expression of the fullness of faith precisely *because* of its original universal character, and its determination to honour both the Eastern and Western expressions of Christianity."

He sees St. John the Baptist Shrine, the sole Ukrainian Catholic church in the capital, as being well positioned to "go beyond itself" and embrace an "extraordinary mission" in welcoming non-Ukrainians to its fold. "Our Patriarch Sviatoslav Shevchuk has said very clearly that we are to use any language that people need – even Russian!" says Butcher.

"When I was received into the Ukrainian Catholic Church, I didn't know anything about Ukrainian culture. I thought of it first and foremost as a gateway to becoming Byzantine rite. But as soon as I got to know Ukrainian Catholics of Ukrainian origin, I realized that for them to be able to love and respect me, they had to see that I love and respect them. No one likes to feel that they are being used by someone just coming to the church for its sacraments, so to speak, without caring about the history of their oppressed culture and ethnicity. You could never be at home in the community with that attitude because you would essentially be saying, 'I don't and I won't love that which is precious to you: I'm just here to take the things I want, and will leave the rest.' But I decided that I could not only live with this reality; I could – and have – learned to love it," says Butcher, whose six children – four daughters and two sons, born between 1998 and 2006 – have all been baptized and chrismated as Ukrainian Catholics.

"Our parish has a responsibility to preserve and cultivate, at some level, the Ukrainian experience – even if the Second Vatican Council spoke of the importance of Eastern Catholics having their own liturgy, spirituality, theology and canon law, but said nothing about culture and language," says Butcher, whose second book will treat the unique character of Eastern Catholic theology. "But our parish also has the obligation to accommodate non-Ukrainians, so that if many, say, Koreans start attending the church, wishing to become Ukrainian Catholics, they could be served in their language, too. So it's a matter of balancing the preservation of Ukrainian heritage for Ukrainian Canadians with making pastoral gestures to non-Ukrainians to ensure that they feel welcome."

"Roman Catholics don't face that challenge because historically, the Western Church has been multi-ethnic, and the nature of the Latin rite is such that it transcends any one ethnic community – creating a supra-national Church. Yet even in the Byzantine rite, a diversity of languages and cultures have shared the same Liturgy of St. John Chrysostom. The genius of Catholicism is that although Eastern Catholics comprise only 1.5 percent of the Church, their presence represents every ancient liturgical tradition – from the Coptic to the Armenian to the Syriac. The universality of the Catholic Church is that there is true unity in diversity," he explains.

"The reason I became Eastern Catholic is the result of having fallen in love with Orthodox liturgy and spirituality, and of being convicted of the truth of the moral teaching and ecclesiology of Catholicism – a vision of the Church in which there is true unity in diversity, guided by the ministry of the successor of Peter," says Butcher.

"I love the Ukrainian Catholic Church because of the people, because of the beauty that's been cultivated over the centuries, and because of the suffering of its martyrs – perhaps, especially, its spirit of *kenosis,* of self-emptying." Wryly he adds, "Given that Ukrainians and the Ukrainian Catholic Church over the years have suffered so much persecution, and from so many different sides, there's nowhere else to go but up!"

3

Erica van Gulik: Joining a New Army for Salvation

Erica and her husband, Roman, crowned in marriage
by Fr. Stephen Wojcichowsky, former director of the Sheptytsky Institute.

Erica with the S.E.R.V.E. team and Fr. John Sianchuk, CSsR (far left),
at Welcome Home, a ministry of the Yorkton Redemptorists in North Winnipeg.

B ecoming a Ukrainian Catholic and marrying a seminarian wasn't Erica van Gulik's original life plan. Born in Ottawa in 1990, van Gulik attended a Salvation Army church in the city with her family and was active there. At the age of seven, she learned how to play the tenor horn and performed in a band at Sunday worship services. Seven years later, van Gulik became a Salvationist soldier who wore a uniform, forswore drinking, smoking and gambling, and vowed to pray and read the Bible as part of her commitment to the ministry of the Church.

"Everybody knew me and my family," she recalls. While studying biology at the University of Ottawa during the 2008–09 academic year, van Gulik planned to become even more involved in the Salvation Army. "I felt called to serve God and wanted to do that through being a minister," she says.

So she dropped her science studies and entered the theology program at Saint Paul University – not far from the University of Ottawa – in 2009 to fulfill that intention. But the new location opened the door to a new spiritual path.

The Sheptytsky Institute of Eastern Christian Studies was located at the time on the Saint Paul campus. Some of van Gulik's male classmates in the theology program were attending Holy Spirit Ukrainian Catholic Seminary, which was also situated in Ottawa then. In 2010, they invited her to attend services in the Sheptytsky Institute chapel, and then St. John the Baptist Ukrainian Catholic Shrine for Saturday evening vespers. Van Gulik was still also attending the Sunday service at the Salvation Army's Ottawa Citadel in the city's east end. "I spent two years with one foot in each of these traditions, but felt myself increasingly drawn to the Ukrainian Catholic Church," she says. "It was March 2012 when I finally talked to my parents and told them how I was feeling about my faith."

Van Gulik had been taking courses at the Sheptytsky Institute and felt that she also had a "solid foundation" on the theological side of the Ukrainian Catholic Church, beyond her growing spiritual connection to it. But she met resistance from members of her Salvation Army community. "They had a hard time with my decision and wanted me to take my time to make sure I was making the right one," recalls van Gulik, whose mother was baptized as a Roman Catholic before joining the Salvation Army as a young adult.

"I was studying theology at a point when I was looking at my faith and what I believed and wanted to know where that belief came from. I was confronted with a Catholicism that seemed to follow a traditional, ritualistic approach to faith in a way that I had never seen before. I had been told that Catholics were not real Christians. The perception was that they go to church – maybe just at Christmas and Easter – and have these rituals but don't actually live their faith in their lives."

She acknowledges that her initial experience attending a Divine Liturgy at the Sheptytsky Institute celebrated by its then-director, Fr. Stephen Wojcichowsky, was "very challenging" and somewhat perplexing. "I was given this book to follow and tried to sing, because I can read music, but it felt almost cultish to me," van Gulik recalls. "They sang everything, there was incense and all sorts of things that I never experienced as part of my worship before. For me, it was like a shock."

"But I kept going to services, because my friends were going, and slowly I got to know the tradition and prayers, and fell in love with the beauty of the liturgy and the depth of the theology. My tradition felt empty as a result because there wasn't any depth. We had no sacraments in the Salvation Army, and I wasn't even baptized as a child. I didn't even know that churches other than the Catholic Church had Baptism or Holy Communion."

"I realized – and believed – that the Eucharist was the Body and Blood of Christ and I wanted to receive it. Not being Catholic, I was barred from it; and it was a really difficult thing for me to long for it and not be able to receive it. So I think that's what finally pushed me to make a decision and move from a faith group that was anti-liturgical to one that is completely liturgical."

In January of 2013, van Gulik received chrismation at St. John the Baptist and became Ukrainian Catholic. At the time, she was in the first year of a two-year Master of Arts program in theology at Saint Paul University. Van Gulik, who graduated magna cum laude with a bachelor's degree in theology from the same university in 2012, focused her graduate work on biblical studies. Her thesis reflected her own journey in understanding and appreciating the important role the sacraments serve in the life of the Church. As she explains, "I sought to explore avenues for progress toward ecumenism. The Roman Catholic–Orthodox dialogue, which assumed a sacramental understanding of the Church, was able to reach a greater degree of consensus with this common starting point, as compared with Evangelicals and Catholics, who do not share such a view. That has made agreement more difficult in the area of ecclesiology."

"More discussion regarding the role of biblical interpretation in ecumenical dialogues would be worthwhile, especially around the acceptance of a sacramental body of Christ. If the Evangelicals, like the Methodists, could appreciate the value in a sacramental interpretation through further joint exploration of the biblical image of the body of Christ, particularly around discussion of 1 Corinthians 11:26 ('For whenever you eat this bread and drink this cup, you proclaim the Lord's death until he comes') and the intimate connection between word and sacrament, there is opportunity for greater convergence on what it means to be the Church."

There was also an opportunity for greater convergence within the Ukrainian Catholic Church for her personally. In 2016, she met her future husband, Roman Kobyletsky, a Ukrainian Catholic from Lviv.

During their honeymoon, they took a high-speed train from Paris to Lourdes, which at first struck van Gulik as a "Catholic Disneyland," with the Virgin Mary's face appearing on an assortment of souvenirs sold in shops throughout the southwestern French town. But the visit to Lourdes, which she found immersed in a prayerful atmosphere, also gave her some insight into her own spiritual struggle with Mary's role in the faith. "I had tried to sort through Marian doctrine and figure out how to make that a part of my faith because praying to Mary for her intercession doesn't come naturally to me."

However, van Gulik says that she had a major intellectual "aha! moment" when she took a course on the seven ecumenical councils at the Sheptytsky Institute and learned about Mary as Theotokos, or God-bearer. "You can't separate the human from the divine nature of Christ, so if Mary is Jesus' mother, she also has to be the Mother of God. I needed to accept the logic of that title," explains van Gulik. "I could then see where that would be a big deal for Catholics, and not just viewing Mary as this young, unimportant girl that God just happened to use and who, after giving birth to Christ, had finished her job."

The Mariological revelation was the final piece of the Eastern Catholic theological puzzle van Gulik needed to resolve in her mind.

She had less trouble embracing the liturgical aspects of the faith.

One of the first services she attended at St. John the Baptist Shrine was the Great Canon of St. Andrew of Crete, held on the fifth Wednesday of Great Lent. "It was a four-hour service with over 200 prostrations – I couldn't walk for two days," recalls van Gulik. "It was one of my most memorable experiences. It was so prayerful, too. Even though I was in so much pain, it was very meditative as we were praying, 'Have mercy on me, O God, have mercy on me.'"

During Holy Week and Easter in the year prior to her chrismation, she went to every Ukrainian Catholic service on the church calendar, including the 5 a.m. Easter Sunday matins at Holy Spirit Seminary; she also attended the Good Friday and Easter Sunday services at her Salvation Army church.

The multi-sensory experience of seeing the majestic icons, hearing the sorrow and joy in the Passion and Paschal music, smelling the burning incense and candles, tasting the blessed Easter food and "touching God" through the mystical worship services helped convince van Gulik that she would mark and celebrate future Easters and holy days in the Ukrainian Catholic tradition.

The Kobyletskys moved to Alberta in January 2019, but van Gulik, who left her job as office manager at Christian Counselling

Ottawa, hopes to bring some influences from her Ukrainian Catholic experience in the national capital out West.

"I would like other Ukrainian Catholic churches to be able to grow the way the one in Ottawa has. But I'm worried that it's not ever going to be replicated anywhere else," she explains. In her opinion, the singularity of the Shrine is its people. "Part of what really made me feel welcome in the church was the community that made me feel part of something in a way I had never felt in the church I grew up in," says van Gulik, who served as the Shrine's parish youth leader from 2014 to 2017.

"It was there that I met people who had similar interests and values as me, who lived those values, and wanted to talk about them and make them a part of their everyday lives. That was something I was looking for all my life and was happy to find in the St. John the Baptist community."

4

Pascal Bastien: An Internist Ventures Further Out

The Bastien family after Liturgy at their new parish,
St. Elias Church in Brampton, Ontario.

Dr. Pascal and Amie Bastien with their children during the blessing of an icon,
"Healer Saint – East and West," that they commissioned for the
Catholic Physicians Guild Congress in May 2019. The icon, blessed
by Fr. Peter Galadza, now hangs in the Sheptytsky Institute Chapel.

For most of his life, Pascal Bastien has been a bit of an outlier – from attending Eastern Orthodox services as a Roman Catholic during his undergraduate university days in Ottawa to preserving his Franco-Canadian heritage by speaking only French to his two young sons and daughter in Toronto, which the family calls home. Attending a Ukrainian Catholic church in Brampton, Ontario, with his children and wife, Amie, an Oshawa, Ontario–born Presbyterian of Vietnamese background and a former investment advisor, is therefore not out of character.

However, these choices aren't about finding a way to be different. They reveal how Bastien – a young blond-and-blue-eyed doctor with a large, outgoing personality that complements his six-foot-four frame – has journeyed on a path to belong. Faith and foundation are important to him, both professionally – as a physician – and personally, as a husband, father and someone who long searched for a spiritual home.

Born in Ottawa in 1982, Bastien was the youngest of three children raised in a French-Canadian home. His father, Richard, is an economist; his mother, Louise, studied psychology before dedicating herself to raising the children.

At the age of 14, Bastien accompanied his parents to Paris, where his dad had been sent by the Canadian government to head Canada's official delegation to the Paris Club, an informal group of official creditors who help debtor countries deal with payment difficulties. Bastien lived with his parents in the French capital for three years; he found his time there transformative. "It was definitely instrumental in helping me shape my understanding of the world, and of God and faith," he recalls of that teenage period in his life where new friendships with peers from different backgrounds opened him up to new ideas.

Those new experiences continued when Bastien returned home and pursued a Bachelor of Applied Sciences degree in computer engineering at the University of Ottawa. Many of the students enrolled in the program were devout Eastern Christians from the

Middle East. "I gravitated toward these colleagues who took their faith seriously, and they became friends of mine," he says.

Bastien would spend his Friday evenings with a Melkite youth group, where he first met Fr. Peter Galadza, who was a guest speaker one evening. On Saturday nights, Bastien would regularly attend midnight praises at a Coptic church. "I discovered things that were very foreign to my experience of prayer and liturgy."

He was intrigued. But then something transformative happened. The World Youth Day cross was winding its way across Canada in advance of Pope John Paul II's historic presence at the Toronto event in July 2002, and made a stop at St. John the Baptist Ukrainian Catholic Shrine in Ottawa, where Great Vespers were held to mark the occasion. Bastien was there.

"Without wanting to sound clichéd, I felt like the emissaries of Prince Vladimir of Kyiv who, after visiting the Hagia Sophia basilica in Constantinople, reported back that they didn't know whether they were in heaven or on earth. That was definitely how I felt," he explains. "At St. John the Baptist, I discovered that praying can be both profound and truly enjoyable – and I wasn't able to get that out of my mind."

Bastien began attending Saturday vespers at the Shrine, where he developed friendships with fellow parishioners who had also come from different faith backgrounds to join the church as Ukrainian Catholics. "I had never before encountered such a warm, familial and welcoming atmosphere," he recalls. "My friendships grew – and with them, my spiritual life."

"The various traditions of the Ukrainian Catholic Church resonated with me – from the smell of the incense to the musical tradition to the beauty of the iconography, the vestments of the priests, and the orientation and structure of the liturgy. It made sense, and felt to me that it was all pointing in the right direction – not so much that God was coming down to us, which in a way he does – but that we were being elevated to witness, to participate in the celestial realm, the heavenly Jerusalem, as theologians would describe it, a closeness with God." Bastien credits his initial encounter with Ukrainian Catholicism as providing him with relief from a "period of drought" he was experiencing at the time in his Christian faith. "It gave me new air to breathe."

He joined St. John the Baptist as a parishioner, around the same time another Roman Catholic, and now a Ukrainian Catholic deacon, Andrew Bennett, became a member. But Bastien did not require a canonical transfer to become Ukrainian Catholic until his first son, Éli, was born in October 2014. The Bastiens wanted him, and any future children, to be baptized and raised as Ukrainian Catholics.

Bastien contacted Cardinal Thomas Collins, the Roman Catholic Archbishop of Toronto – as a member of the Toronto Catholic Doctors' Guild, he knew the Cardinal personally – to request that he be officially released from the Latin rite. Once that was granted, Bastien received approval from Bishop Stephen Chmilar, the Ukrainian Catholic Eparch of Toronto, to become Ukrainian Catholic.

Subsequently, his children have been baptized at St. Elias the Prophet Church in Brampton, the Ukrainian Catholic parish the Bastiens attend as a family. Although Amie has remained a Protestant, she is "happy to raise our children in the Ukrainian Catholic Church with me," says Bastien.

In light of the couple's mixed faith communities, the family alternates between attending Sunday service at a Presbyterian church, where Amie receives Communion, and St. Elias for the English-language Divine Liturgy on Sundays, where Pascal and their children receive. "Amie has definitely felt a sense of spiritual growth through belonging to St. Elias and that her Christian experience would not be complete if she only went to a Presbyterian church. But she needs both," explains Bastien, who notes that his wife is an active parishioner at St. Elias and serves as a bell-ringer. The family also attends Saturday vespers at St. Elias.

"My marriage to a woman who is Protestant has forced me out of a certain closed mind-frame that I was in before," says Bastien. "And I certainly believe that God uses Amie and my exposure to very holy Protestants that I encounter to teach me many things about faith. As a Ukrainian Catholic, I have tons to learn from the Protestant experience – their better knowledge of Scripture, their great zeal and burning desire that the world come to know Jesus Christ, their very well thought-out plan to raise children in the faith and come to know the Bible at home and at church in an organized way."

Still, he feels most at home at St. Elias and, when in Ottawa, St. John the Baptist, where both parishes have been most welcoming to Bastien and his family. It certainly helps that both churches hold services in English and not exclusively in Ukrainian, a language Bastien does not understand with any fluency. To his credit, however, he masterfully pronounces a long list of Ukrainian words he has acquired along the way.

He believes that setting foot in other Ukrainian Catholic churches that focus on Ukrainian exclusively in their liturgical and social practices would leave him feeling like an outsider. "I see that not as a failure of the Ukrainian Greco-Catholic Church, but as a failure of members of our Church to understand what the Church is about," Bastien says.

"It took me 15 years to start understanding why many Eastern Churches have a strong, often isolating ethnic focus. But it's a fact that Ukraine and the Ukrainian language were suppressed under the Soviets, and outside Ukraine, Ukrainians felt it was their mission, their mandate to protect their culture that had been oppressed. Since they were already organized around a Church community, and since seeking independence from Communism is a noble ideal, it may have been natural to see this as an extension of this Christian community's mandate."

"But that also meant that the Church – a place where, first and foremost, people from all backgrounds should be invited to encounter Jesus Christ – could be hijacked to serve a secular, albeit very positive, cultural focus."

Bastien also points to examples where Ukrainian Canadians have been impressed, if not amazed, at his enthusiasm for being a Ukrainian Catholic. "Two physicians involved with me in the Toronto Catholic Doctors' Guild, who are both Ukrainian, have been attending Roman Catholic parishes for the last 10 years in one case, and 20 years, in the other," says Bastien. "They left their Ukrainian Catholic parishes because, like many second- and third-generation Ukrainian Canadians, they felt a linguistic and cultural gap with the Church of their forefathers. So you can imagine their surprise when they learned that I – this French-Canadian guy – am not only attending a Ukrainian Catholic church, but am happy to talk cheerfully about how much I love the Ukrainian Catholic Church and how it has helped me become closer to Jesus Christ. It was a huge shock for them."

Bastien is, as he acknowledges, an extrovert; he is highly animated when he talks about Ukrainian Catholicism and confesses to having more passion discussing it than, say, some article in *The New England Journal of Medicine*. That's not to suggest that his career is not important to him. After graduating with a medical degree from the University of Ottawa in 2008, Bastien completed his specialty training in internal medicine and a sub-specialty, general internal medicine, at the University of Toronto. He now heads the division of general internal medicine at Toronto's North York General Hospital, and has published peer-reviewed articles in the area of venous thromboembolism. But for him, faith is "more life-changing," and "heals more than just an organ for a little bit of time."

"Modern man has reached great levels of scientific knowledge and the general population has access to a high level of education compared to our ancestors. The notion of the fisherman blindly accepting faith – as beautiful and pure as it may be – is becoming increasingly elusive," Bastien explains.

"We are going to be challenged, first within our own hearts and also unavoidably by others, and this can be a very good thing. It certainly forces us out of a lukewarm state, and can be an impetus to grow in faith. Christians ought to embrace science fearlessly and enthusiastically. God cannot contradict reason because he is the source of reason, and thus faith cannot but be in harmony with reason."

"I live in downtown Toronto, so I can assure you I encounter many who suggest that science has triumphed over religion, and don't shy away from affirming that anything we perceive above the physical realm is, at its core, delusional. But I would argue here, as I often do professionally in the clinical realm, that a little knowledge is worse than none. I find very few people actually interested or capable of defending that position," says Bastien.

"Throughout my engineering and medical studies, and still now in my workplace, I find that the obstacles to faith have much more to do with personal situations than an assent to, say, a materialist philosophy, such as Richard Dawkins' superficially popular writings. These personal situations vary and can range from a life without any suffering where God seems unnecessary, to a life with suffering where there is bewilderment at the great question of human suffering and anger at God."

"In any case, I think it is important for Christians of all times not only to be engaged in their faith in the spiritual realm, but also to have both feet in the *hic et nunc*, addressing current concerns and witnessing to their contemporaries," Bastien explains.

"I was both touched and saddened when, recently, one of my atheist Jewish colleagues said to me, 'Pascal, you're the first practising Christian I know whom I have intellectual respect for.' For him, people of faith had appeared as people who shut their brain off."

"There is also a limit to our human understanding of God, and that very point has allowed me to grow. I have come to appreciate greatly the apophatic emphasis of the Eastern tradition, which embraces the notion of God as mystery, of God beyond understanding."

Through the Toronto Catholic Doctors' Guild, the young internist is regularly involved in various evenings of prayer and fellowship with medical trainees and fellow Christian physicians. He sees this as an important aspect of his prayer life, and feels it is all the more relevant given growing pressures within his field to embrace professional values that are at odds with the Gospel.

Thus, Bastien's focus is on the spiritual aspect of the Church, and not on the cultural appendage that can come along with it. "I have a lot of love for Ukrainians and Ukrainian culture," he explains. "But my becoming Ukrainian Catholic has nothing to do with trying to be Ukrainian – by acquiring fluency in the language, for instance. It has everything to do with having a connection to the spiritual heritage of the Church of Kyiv. It has to do with being closer to Jesus Christ."

"If joining our Church means I ought to learn Ukrainian, what happens to the next French Canadian, or someone of Chinese or Portuguese ethnicity, who walks into the parish? Might they not be tempted to think I belong because I am fluent in Ukrainian but that they don't belong? And isn't the same true of the children of Ukrainian Catholics who are out of touch with the 'motherland' and no longer attend our churches?"

Says Bastien: "I am very happy to be this kind of rebellious witness. If, like me, you feel called to grow spiritually in this Church, then this is your home – and it doesn't matter at all if you don't speak Ukrainian."

Still on the matter of languages, he says he has been overjoyed to work with the liturgical commission of the Ukrainian Catholic Eparchy in Paris to adapt existing French liturgical texts to the specific usage and musical tradition of the Ukrainian Church. Bastien hopes the use of these French texts will allow fellow French speakers to discover the spiritual treasures of the Kyivan Church. He also aspires to be ordained a reader, and hopes that it may become commonplace for parishes in French territories to sing troparia or read the Epistle in French – as, for example, at St. John the Baptist in Ottawa, where several new parishioners are Francophones.

"I'm a stubborn guy, and while we live in Toronto, Amie and I only speak French to our children at home – and our eldest is unilingual French," says Bastien. "That paradoxically forces me to have an understanding of Ukrainians who want to give a lot of importance to the Ukrainian language. It reminds me acutely that while French is beautiful, it is not more important than the faith. The Church can never be an ethnic club."

For Bastien, Ukrainian Catholicism has brought him "joy, love, meaning, direction – but above all, joy."

"My faith has been able to resonate with previously unfound vigour, which I attribute to the richness and treasures of the Church of Kyiv. Without it, I am unaware of any other way by which I could have this relationship with Christ."

5

Andrew Bennett: Journeying from Public Service to Serving the Church

Andrew Bennett is presented for ordination to the diaconate by
Protodeacon David Kennedy at St. John the Baptist Ukrainian Catholic Shrine.

Bennett as Canada's Ambassador for Religious Freedom with
Coptic Archbishop Angaelos, presently of London, UK, in St. Peter's Basilica
during a conference on persecuted Christians called "Under Caesar's Sword."

Urbane and whip-smart, Andrew Bennett could have easily risen up the ranks of Canada's public service – or perhaps obtained a plum diplomatic posting – while remaining a Roman Catholic as he was raised in Toronto.

As Canada's first, and so far only, ambassador for religious freedom who has held senior positions in the federal government and who holds a Ph.D. in political science, Bennett boasts a star-quality CV that allows him to call the shots for future employment. He could have entered politics and run for office – and likely would have won, as a Liberal or a Conservative, and taken a seat in the House of Commons. But Bennett's past inclinations were to play a behind-the-scenes role in policy-making rather than serve as an elected politician involved in applying policy to government legislation.

His present inclinations are decidedly different. Bennett's notion of public service is now religious, not political – as a Ukrainian Catholic planning to serve his Church as a priest. "For this kind of WASP-y guy from Toronto, the Ukrainian Catholic Church is where the Holy Spirit has called me to be," he explains.

Born in Canada's largest city in 1972, Bennett attended Our Lady of Perpetual Help Church, a Roman Catholic parish in Toronto's St. Clair–Mount Pleasant neighbourhood. His parents were married at Perpetual Help, and he was baptized and celebrated his Confirmation and First Communion there. Bennett's boyhood faith was emboldened by his deeply religious Irish-Catholic mom and Scottish-Catholic dad – and it made an impression on him. "I was a pretty churchy kid," he recalls. "I loved going to church and being involved in church-related things. Naturally, I was an altar boy."

There were early signs that a clerical vocation lay in his future. "At the age of seven or eight, I wanted to be a priest," says Bennett. "My cousins and I would take Wonder Bread and press it down into little hosts. But our 'Mass' lasted all of three minutes, after which we munched on our Wonder Bread hosts."

"I remember when I was nine going to visit my maternal grandparents who lived in the same part of Toronto as we did, and my grandfather asking me, 'What do you want to be when you grow up?' Without hesitation I said, 'a priest.' This call would come and go. I think our Lord is very patient and gave me opportunities to explore other areas of interest." He did, but there was always a religious underlay in his life.

However, Bennett was not schooled in the Catholic tradition. From grades five to 13, he attended an Anglican boys' private school – the prestigious Royal St. George's College – which required his wearing a uniform and his parents sacrificing much to pay the hefty tuition. "It was one of the greatest gifts they gave me," he says. The experience resulted in lifelong friendships and a focus for his higher education. At St. George's, Bennett excelled in French, Latin, music, history and political science, and pursued the humanities in university.

In 1995, he obtained a Bachelor of Arts in history, with first-class honours, from Dalhousie University in Halifax. Two years later, Bennett graduated from Montreal's McGill University with a Master of Arts in history.

At that point, he considered going to law school. But after sharing that idea with one of his best friends, Bennett realized that he couldn't just study constitutional law – his true passion – but would have to immerse himself in much drier courses on contract law and torts as well. So, he opted for the doctoral route. Bennett crossed the Atlantic and headed for the land of his paternal forefathers to enroll at the University of Edinburgh. There, he worked on his thesis: "Nations of Distinction: Nationalist Attitudes to Constitutional Change in Scotland, Quebec and Catalunya."

Bennett sought to explain how federalist states, like Canada, attempt to accommodate claims for greater autonomy from, in its case, Quebec and its historic quest for nationhood within the confederation. His research resulted in a Ph.D. in politics, awarded to him in 2002, after he had landed an exciting job back home in Canada.

In May 2001, Bennett joined the Privy Council Office (PCO) in Ottawa, where he applied his academic work to political parliamentary action. As a policy analyst, the former member of the Young Liberals of Canada conducted research on comparative constitutional models and federal systems to support the then-intergovernmental affairs minister, Stéphane Dion, following the passing into law of the *Clarity Act* regarding Quebec secession in June 2000.

However, the University of Edinburgh experience did not just lead Bennett into a public policy career. His time on the Scottish campus had also whetted his appetite for Eastern Christianity. "I was involved in the Catholic Students' Union, and there was a small Orthodox chaplaincy that I tried to do some ecumenical work with," says Bennett, who notes that his prayer life "matured and deepened" while he was in Edinburgh.

Contact with the Orthodox reminded him of his first taste of the Eastern Christian tradition when, as a teenager and his parents were away for the weekend, he decided to attend Sunday Divine Liturgy at Holy Eucharist Ukrainian Catholic Church in down-town Toronto. "I knew it was Catholic, so I could receive Holy Communion," explains Bennett. "And something was awakened in me spiritually by the Byzantine liturgy."

In Ottawa, while working at the PCO, Bennett became a parishioner at Notre Dame Cathedral in Ottawa. He joined the choir and participated in a parish group for young professionals, through which he attended World Youth Day in July 2002 in his hometown, Toronto. Saint Pope John Paul II was there, too, and Bennett remembers feeling that he was in the presence of a "great and saintly man."

"It really had a profound impact on me, and I came away from World Youth Day with a love for our Lord, a love for the Church, and a love for the Holy Father, and realized that I needed to pursue my vocational discernment in a much more concerted fashion," Bennett explains. "John Paul II's infirmity laid bare that despite his physical limitations and suffering, he was a great witness to the dignity of the human person and the value of life in all forms."

Through the fall of 2002, Bennett met with Jesuit, Dominican and diocesan priests in Ottawa to discuss his interest in pursuing the priesthood. He gave himself one year to decide whether he would leave the PCO and enter the seminary. But Bennett abandoned the timeline before the year ended. His decision had nothing to do with his career in the government, which was moving along nicely; he was promoted to the position of senior policy analyst and research coordinator for Infrastructure Canada's then cities secretariat. Bennett put his plan for the priesthood on ice because of a crisis of faith. "In late 2002 and early 2003, I experienced what I would call a fairly deep spiritual malaise where my prayer life dried up," he recalls. "I wasn't praying daily; I wasn't even saying grace before meals. It wasn't a loss of faith. It was just that my spiritual life was very dry."

"I would go to Mass frustrated with why the priest was doing what he was doing, with the felt banners – and I felt that the choir really sucked. I didn't understand at the time why I was feeling this. I hadn't had an experience like that before. But in hindsight, I think our Lord was giving me a taste of spiritual suffering, of spiritual malaise – and was allowing me to experience that call to me to persevere. And I did. I continued to go to Mass."

Bennett's spiritual drought ended through a work connection. A female colleague of his at the PCO, with whom he was close, invited him to accompany her to the Dormition of the Virgin Mary Greek Orthodox Church that she attended in Ottawa. They went to the Sunday morning Divine Liturgy, and would continue to do so every week for several months. In the evening, Bennett would go to Blessed Sacrament, a Roman Catholic parish he belonged to at the time, for the Sunday evening Mass to receive the Eucharist. His friend was oblivious to the spiritual struggle he was experiencing.

"In early February 2003, I told her about this Ukrainian Catholic church I discovered where I could go to Communion and she could have her Byzantine liturgy," Bennett recalls. On the pre-Lent Cheesefare Sunday, the pair went to St. John the Baptist Ukrainian Catholic Shrine. "There were wonderful people, a wonderful liturgy in English, wonderful singing, and I thought, wow, this is great," Bennett says. Reading the church bulletin, he noticed that the parish served the Divine Liturgy of the Presanctified Gifts during Great Lent, and was intrigued. "I thought that sounded interesting and wanted to come back for that," continued Bennett, who returned to the Shrine for the liturgy.

Meanwhile, his friend moved to Toronto and pursued a relationship with another man, leaving Bennett heartbroken. But he continued going to St. John the Baptist, and quickly formed friendships with other non-Ukrainian parishioners, such as Harold and Rebecca Visser and Pascal Bastien – as Bennett described them, the "non-Uke super-Ukes" who have wholly embraced Ukrainian Catholicism as part of their lives.

Fr. Michael Winn, the rector of Holy Spirit Ukrainian Catholic Seminary – located in Ottawa at the time – gave him books to read on Byzantine spiritual and liturgical traditions. "After about four months, my spiritual malaise was gone," explains Bennett, who shortly thereafter enrolled at the Sheptytsky Institute of Eastern Christian Studies and studied theology part-time.

"I had acquired this strength in my prayer life and a greater love for the Eucharist – both the precious body and the blood of Christ – to the point where I was craving it." Bennett began regularly attending Saturday evening vespers and the Sunday morning English-language liturgy at St. John the Baptist. As he explains, his priestly vocation returned with "greater strength and greater clarity."

"There was always this knocking at the door of my heart, and our Lord was always there kind of saying, 'Will you now say yes to what I'm calling you to be?'"

First, Bennett needed to join the Ukrainian Catholic Church. In 2005, he petitioned Bishop Stephan Chmilar of the Eparchy of Toronto and Eastern Canada to transfer his ascription from the Roman Catholic Church to the Ukrainian Catholic Church. The change of rite was approved; Bennett became a parishioner at St. John the Baptist Shrine and started to think seriously about his vocation.

By this time, Bennett had left the PCO and joined Export Development Canada (EDC), where he worked as a senior political risk analyst and managed the file for Europe and Central Asia, with a focus on Ukraine, Russia, Turkey, Kazakhstan and Kyrgyzstan. In December 2009, he decided the time was right to pursue his vocation. He took a leave of absence from his job at EDC and entered Holy Spirit Seminary.

But Bennett was only there for six months. "I wasn't prepared to be ordained a priest yet and had the sense that there was something else I was called to do," he says. That something involved the establishment of a new diplomatic post by the federal government, and Bennett knew the man behind the idea.

In 2001, he had met Jason Kenney, the current premier of Alberta. At the time, Kenney was a member of Parliament with the Canadian Alliance, a former conservative party that served as the Official Opposition in the House of Commons. A decade later, Bennett attended the National Prayer Breakfast in Ottawa and ran into Kenney, who by then was in government, serving as the minister of citizenship and immigration with responsibility for multiculturalism. The two agreed to meet for coffee. Kenney asked Bennett his thoughts on the government's plan, led by Kenney, to create an office of religious freedom. "I told him that to be totally honest, I hadn't heard about it, but it sounded like a good idea," recalls Bennett.

Later in the fall of 2011, the two men met up again, this time at a symposium at Saint Paul University on the future of Christianity in the Middle East. Kenney provided more detail on the proposed religious freedom office that would be run through the Department of Foreign Affairs, Trade and Development (DFAIT; it was renamed Global Affairs Canada in 2015). Bennett told the minister that he would be interested in getting involved in such an initiative.

More than a year passed before Bennett heard any news. But in December 2012 Kenney contacted him, telling him that the government was proceeding with launching the Office of Religious Freedom (ORF) in February 2013. "Jason said, 'We'd like you to be a part of it,' and I said, 'In a policy capacity?'" recalls Bennett. "And he said, 'No, Andrew, we're putting your name forward to the prime minister to be appointed as the first ambassador.' And I thought, wow!"

On February 19, 2013, Bennett was appointed Canada's first ambassador for religious freedom and head of the ORF within DFAIT. He led a team of six public servants in an office with an annual budget of $5 million, most of which was directed to a religious freedom fund that supported more than 20 international projects in 10 countries and regions, including Ukraine, to advance freedom of religion or belief.

Under Bennett's watch, in June 2015, an international contact group on freedom of religion or belief was also established. It brought together the foreign ministries of 25 nations to champion actions aimed at improving global religious freedom. The office became "a centrepiece of foreign policy" for the federal Conservative government, but the opposition Liberal party was "allergic" to its purpose, according to Bennett.

When Justin Trudeau's Liberals formed the government following the 2015 federal election, the Office of Religious Freedom's days were numbered. In May 2016, Stéphane Dion, whom Trudeau named as his first foreign affairs minister and for whom Bennett had once worked, announced that the office would be replaced with a new Office of Human Rights, Freedoms and Inclusion. It would operate with an annual budget of $15 million, three times the amount the Harper government allocated for the ORF.

Bennett says the Liberal government's decision to end the ORF's mandate "demonstrated poor thinking" and a "fairly naïve view that you can advance the human rights of all at the same time." That idea flows from a "philosophical view that doesn't believe that religion should be discussed within foreign policy, let alone public policy."

"Sometimes, you need to amplify a particular human right if there's a need," says Bennett, who two months prior to the ORF's closing joined the faith-based think tank Cardus as a senior fellow. "You can have an office of religious freedom, because religious persecution is a serious issue in much of the world. But that doesn't mean you don't talk about freedom of the press, or freedom of expression or women's rights. In Canada, we have long had a minister of state responsible for the status of women because there are still issues of pay equity and other issues."

Bennett, who describes himself on Wikipedia as a "public intellectual" and in conversation as a "Burkean conservative wrapped up in a 1950 European Christian Democrat," is nonetheless a nonpartisan who has voted for every major party in Canada, including the Greens. He also acknowledges the separation between church and state. "If you think that a political party is there to advance the Gospel, that's really naïve. It's there to gain power and advance a political program," he says. "As the psalmist says, 'put not your trust in princes.' The role of Christians is to proclaim the Gospel to the world."

As the first and possibly last Canadian ambassador for religious freedom, Bennett continues the work he began in that role. He is a senior fellow with the Washington, D.C.–based Religious Freedom Institute (RFI), whose aim is to achieve broad acceptance of religious liberty as a fundamental human right. He also plays a major role at Cardus' office in Ottawa, serving as both director of the Cardus Religious Freedom Institute – a Canadian offshoot of the American Religious Freedom Institute – and program director of Cardus Law, whose mandate is to "foster emerging scholarship, facilitate public discussion and engage legal processes without intervening to uphold the belief that the law serves society, thereby enabling human flourishing and the advancement of the common good."

Bennett deeply believes that everyone should have the freedom to worship in any faith and the right to not have any faith. He also deeply believes in his faith as he moves closer to the priesthood. In 2017, he was ordained to the diaconate at St. John the Baptist Shrine on November 30 – the feast day of St. Andrew, the apostle Bennett is named after, who is also the patron saint of Ukraine and fishermen (Bennett likes to fly fish). Saint Andrew's Day is, of course, commemorated annually in Scotland as its national holiday.

As a Ukrainian Catholic deacon, Bennett has been leading the Saturday evening vespers at the church and assisting at the English-language Divine Liturgy on Sunday mornings and feast days. Although his Ukrainian vocabulary is limited ("I cannot yet string together a conversation in Ukrainian"), he can read enough of the language to lead the congregation in prayer.

Bennett admits that when he started attending services at St. John the Baptist, his presence there piqued the curiosity of long-time parishioners. "I was asked, 'Why are you in this church?' and I would say I am here because the Holy Spirit has led me here. Someone like me, who is not ethnically Ukrainian but is part of the Church, has to have a love for its Kyivan-Galician Byzantine tradition." He says that love has only grown as he has learned more about the history of the Church, particularly during the 20th century, as it led its followers in Ukraine through the horrors of the Holodomor and the Second World War, and the Church's own suppression under decades of Soviet rule.

"Because the Church has been such a faithful witness, the key element of its mission in the world is union – to try to heal the divisions between East and West," explains Bennett. "Ukrainian Catholics have often been given the supposedly derogatory epithet as 'Uniates' – that somehow we're sellouts to Orthodoxy. But if a Uniate is someone desiring unity, then call me a Uniate! I'll wear the label proudly."

"The Church faces many struggles of not being understood by the West and its fellow Orthodox followers – and we are an ortho-dox Church. So we live in this in-between space, which I think is a wonderful place to be. It gives you a certain freedom," says Bennett, an avid reader of the Church Fathers, including Saints Maximus the Confessor and John Chrysostom. "We live out our Orthodox spirituality, but in union with the See of Rome; we can swim in a broader sea of the Western tradition and inform it by our Eastern life, but also receive what is good from that tradition and understand it through an Eastern lens."

Bennett, who taught a course on the history of Christianity at Augustine College – a private, non-denominational Christian, one-year liberal arts post-secondary institution in Ottawa – believes that while the Ukrainian Catholic Church has its roots in Kyivan Rus' dating back to 988, when Vladimir the Great embraced Eastern Christianity, and has been geographically situated in what is now Ukraine for more than a millennium, it is "not a Church just for Ukrainians."

"The Church can never be just for one people. The Church is for all people," he says. "The Church is first and foremost evangelical – it is to be brought to all people. And what a wonderful gift it is to bring our Eastern Byzantine faith through the Ukrainian tradition to the world."

"I am never going to be Ukrainian; I don't want to be Ukrainian. I am who I am – although we have a common love of root vegetables," he laughs. "I am proud to be a guy with a Scottish-Irish background."

"If I were Ukrainian, I would think, wow, these non-Ukrainian people want to be in this Church that has suffered, that has been victimized and persecuted, and now the Holy Spirit is working in this way to lead these people to our Church. Wow, we must have something really amazing and really special!"

Bennett compares the Ukrainian Catholic Church to how followers of the early Christian Church in Jerusalem felt about Paul welcoming non-Jews (Greeks) into the fold. "I think we have to look at it through that light," he says. "We're not just the Church of 'the Jews' – or Ukrainians in this case – but the Church of 'the gentiles' – non-Ukrainians – too."

"We are the Church of the Irish and Scottish, of French Canadians, and Koreans and the Dutch – all of these people who are coming to St. John the Baptist. It's interesting that our Church, which came to Canada, now has all these people from different ethnic backgrounds who have found our Church. If that's not the work of the Holy Spirit, I don't know what is." Says Bennett: "It's faith first, culture second."

The next step in his faith journey will be to complete his theology degree and any time remaining in his seminary formation, and hopefully be ordained to the priesthood. Ordained to the diaconate as a single man, Bennett will have to remain celibate. "I always saw myself as a husband and as a dad, but there is this other calling," says the handsome six-foot-three scholar and former envoy who sports designer glasses. "However, one of our priests once said to me, 'Andrew, a man that can't see himself as a husband and a father has no place in the celibate priesthood.' You're called to be a husband to Christ's bride, the Church, and you're also called to be a father to many people."

For now, he bases his life around the diaconate and preaches the message of the evangelization occurring within the Ukrainian Catholic Church. "It's like in the Gospel of John when John the Baptist sees Jesus and calls him the 'Lamb of God,' and two of John's disciples follow Jesus and ask him where he is staying and Jesus says, 'Come, and you will see.' From an Eastern perspective, our Church says to people, 'come and see the beauty of our liturgy and our spiritual life – the rhythm of feasting and fasting – and be drawn into a beautiful relationship with the holy Trinity,'" explains Bennett. "We always have to be invitational."

He says that Ukrainian Catholicism has brought him a "greater appreciation of beauty." "Beauty is something that God has given us, and the liturgy is the most beautiful thing possible in which God reveals himself. The Byzantine Christian world view is so shaped by beauty, so shaped by the importance of matter. Matter matters, where the unseen God becomes human."

"What we do with matter – creating beautiful things like art and music with our voices – is really essential. The Byzantine tradition does this in a very full way and a very revelatory way that is sometimes lacking in other Christian traditions. I'm so happy where God has brought me."

6

Lisa Gilbert: A Nomadic Doctor "Settles Down"

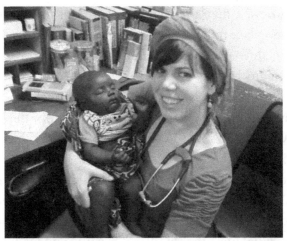

Dr. Lisa Gilbert with one of her young patients in Africa.

Lisa Gilbert in traditional African dress.

Lisa in protective clothing during the Ebola epidemic.

Blessed with a bubbly personality and a deep desire to help others, Lisa Gilbert was destined to work with people on her career path. Gifted with an insatiable curiosity, an unquenchable thirst for knowledge, and a scientific and analytical mind, she chose medicine as a profession.

That vocation, matched with an inherent wanderlust, took Gilbert to various places on the planet where she was exposed to different cultures and beliefs, while helping to save lives. Yet something was missing. Gilbert's heart and mind were fully engaged with the people she worked with and treated. She had faith in God and a love for Christ, but her soul remained restless and hungered for nourishment.

Born to devoutly Evangelical Christian missionary parents in the United States, in her spiritual journey Gilbert followed an unconventional path that began in Africa and ended up taking her to Canada. As a volunteer physician, she provided medical care to Africa's poorest – from dealing with those stricken with the deadly Ebola virus in Liberia to multitasking in emergency care, pediatrics and obstetrics at a 100-bed rural hospital in Niger. More recently, Gilbert worked at a Catholic mission hospital in rural Cameroon through the Mission Doctors Association, a Los Angeles–based non-profit organization that sends Catholic physicians to under-served areas of the world (she is on the board).

Gilbert was already familiar with Africa, having spent much of her childhood there. Growing up in Kenya, where her Pentecostal parents worked as missionaries for the U.S. Assemblies of God, Gilbert went with them to visit an HIV/AIDS orphanage where most of the babies with weakened immune systems died before their fifth birthday. At the age of 10, Gilbert "made a promise to herself: she would go back and work there as an adult." The promise is quoted in a profile of her published in the Catholic Medical Association's *The Pulse of Catholic Medicine* journal (Fall/Winter 2017 issue).

Gilbert could easily have followed the path of her parents. She was born in 1983 in Springfield, Missouri, the Midwestern

American city that is home to the headquarters of the Assemblies of God and where she spent the first three years of her life, before her parents moved Gilbert and her older brother to Kenya.

"My parents are true Evangelical charismatics," says Gilbert. "My father fasts completely from food and drink except water for three 24-hour days every month – usually all at once on a weekend, and he devotes himself to prayer. My mother prays a lot, too, and reads through the entire Bible every year, which she has done for most of her life."

Gilbert recalls that as a child, the first thing she would see when she got up in the morning was her mother sitting in her robe in a chair, reading the Scriptures with curlers in her hair, and praying through her lists of prayer requests or intentions that others had given her.

Gilbert's grandparents were also devout Christians. Her maternal grandparents – former Lutherans who joined the Assemblies of God later in life – "gave out more Bibles than anyone I have ever met," says Gilbert. The familial Christian influence, though strong, was not oppressive. "I led a happy and simple childhood, spending time outside, making crafts or playing with other kids, joyfully free of most modern technology," says Gilbert. "I loved Jesus, my parents and brother, my friends, my hamsters, my cat. As a small child, I liked to make people smile, and would draw or colour pictures for the Bible school students. I loved to write little stories and, most of all, to read. But I was not particularly popular. I was a bit nerdy, physically awkward and chubby; occasionally I think I was also a bit smug and self-righteous, but I think my friends loved me anyway and I didn't have any enemies."

At the age of nine, wearing a pink bathing suit, she was baptized into the Assemblies of God in the Indian Ocean at Mombasa, Kenya. "I can still remember the salty waves going over my head," recalls Gilbert. "As a very symbolic person, I had no doubt in my mind about what I was committing to: to die with Christ and be raised with him and to pledge my loyalty to him for the rest of my life. It has been a commitment I have renewed many times since then – but even at that age, I knew what this meant." She just didn't know at the time how it would be revealed.

Initially, it came through as a sense of service to others, developed while she was living in Africa. "I loved growing up in Kenya and never felt completely at home in the United States," says Gilbert, who returned to the U.S. when her parents were relocated to Lubbock, Texas, during her second- and seventh-grade years, and for six months during her fifth-grade year. She became severely ill with a viral infection: she lost her central vision and required medical treatment to have it restored.

"Lubbock is a smelly, dusty cow-town – with lovely people, of course – but honestly, I really struggled with it after experiencing the beauty of Kenya. And I never felt comfortable there; I had always worn skirts, and in the U.S. girls wore pants and talked about things I didn't understand. My differences were tolerated, and I did have some friends, but I was truly glad to return home to Africa at the end of those two separate years."

Following her seventh-grade year, Gilbert's family moved to Togo, where she attended a British high school. "Most of my classmates were Nigerian and Ghanaian expats, so I was caught between being rich by comparison to the local people at church and perhaps even a bit poorer compared to some of my classmates. Along with that there were the cultural differences between all of us, and Togo itself being a French-speaking country with a variety of cultures, tribes and languages," she says. "But again, I really loved it and had wonderful friends."

After graduating from high school, Gilbert returned to the U.S. and enrolled at Missouri State University (MSU) in Springfield to pursue double-major science degrees in cellular and molecular biology and French. But it wouldn't be long before she was back in Africa. After two years of studies at MSU, Gilbert spent a volunteer year at Nazareth House, a Catholic AIDS orphanage for HIV-positive children in Cape Town, South Africa, where her parents were stationed at the time as missionaries.

As she told *The Pulse of Catholic Medicine*, it was in Cape Town that "she felt like the promise she had made as a child was finally being fulfilled"; she had her first exposure to the Catholic Church there, along with an existential crisis. One baby she got close to died just before Gilbert left South Africa. The little girl's name was Lucinathi, which in Xhosa, one of South Africa's official languages, means "God's blessing is with us."

"God is always with us, even in hard times, but at that moment it felt like God's blessing had vanished because Lucinathi had been taken," Gilbert told the Catholic Medical Association journal. "This was my first experience with injustice and the profoundness of suffering. I never doubted God's existence, but I was dealing with the grief of a broken, fallen world." She would choose to help heal it through medicine.

After graduating magna cum laude with double science degrees from MSU and receiving multiple scholarships for studies in medicine, in 2005, Gilbert attended the University of Texas–Southwestern Medical School in Dallas. She completed her residency in family medicine in 2012 at Via Christi, a Catholic health care services provider in Wichita, Kansas, and spent a year on a fellowship. During that fellowship, she received certification in clinical tropical medicine and traveler's health from West Virginia University School of Medicine. Gilbert also undertook a five-month practicum at a mission hospital in Niger, where she gained experience usually referred to specialists. She worked in an intensive care unit for burn victims, performed caesarean sections and did dentistry.

The work was hard – and emotionally draining. Many of her patients, a lot of them infants, died either during delivery or after contracting malaria. Gilbert needed a break and some healing – of the spiritual kind. The break she chose was both dramatic and life changing.

Until then, Gilbert had remained within the Protestant fold. The born-and-raised Pentecostal spent some time as a young adult "bouncing around" different Christian denominations – Baptist,

Methodist and Presbyterian – before briefly joining a conservative Lutheran church. "Throughout college, medical school and residency, I would often go to various churches just to sit and pray," says Gilbert. "Over time, I could tell there was a difference between those churches that featured the Eucharist in worship services, and those that did not; those that didn't seemed empty to me, and I found myself drawn more and more to Catholic and Orthodox churches."

She believes that attraction was the result of a "profound sense of the spiritual world" acquired from her charismatic upbringing that followed her into adulthood. "When I was in Africa, I could always sense the voodoo presence in some market stalls, even without looking, and I continue to pray in tongues at times, a gift that the Lord gave me as a child," she explains. "I think it was this same sense of the spiritual world that drew me to the real presence of Christ in the Ukrainian Catholic Church."

Gilbert pursued that path when she happened upon the Eighth Day Institute, a faith-and-learning organization primarily targeted to the Catholic-Orthodox community in Wichita, Kansas, where she is based. "I began reading every day about the Church Fathers and Eastern Christian theology and fell in love with it," she says.

"The way the history of Christianity had previously been presented to me was that Christ had, of course, founded the Church. There were the twelve apostles and this initially huge missionary movement that spread rapidly. But over the next several hundred years, pretty much everyone fell into apostasy, which lasted for the next 1,500 years. Then Luther came along and restored the Church, more or less. Calvin tried, too, as did a few others, but they got a lot of things wrong in the process. The Church continued to smoulder in residual ritualistic dead practices, left over from Catholicism, for the next 400 years until there was this new Pentecostal movement when the Holy Spirit finally showed up again. Now the Church is being restored back to the way it was in the Book of Acts through the Assemblies of God. Although not quite as succinct, this was essentially what was taught to me through sermons and readings."

What struck Gilbert was that none of the Protestant churches she examined "believe or even know what the Early Church actually taught. It was amazing to me that the earliest documents by the immediate successors of the Apostles taught things that we moderns believe today about the sacraments – about the Eucharist, baptism, about almost all the fundamental things of our faith." However, she was impressed by how Eastern Catholicism focused on the importance of the sacraments as a way to achieve "theosis – that is, deification – or union with Christ." But Gilbert had never set foot in an Eastern Catholic church until she came to Ottawa in 2013.

While attending medical school in Dallas, Gilbert met John Patrick, a retired British-born physician who established Augustine College, a non-denominational, one-year liberal arts college, in Ottawa in 1997. Gilbert decided to take a year off from medicine and use that sabbatical to study philosophy, theology, Church history and Greek for two semesters at Augustine College (she flew back to Kansas several times to fill in as an emergency physician at a rural hospital). The break allowed her to regroup mentally.

Gilbert had just finished her second tour of duty at the mission hospital in Niger: at the time she was there, it was ranked as the worst in the world for maternal and child care. "I saw a lot of death and needed healing from that," she explains. "I had also thought about going overseas permanently with an Evangelical missions agency, but I knew I couldn't because I still felt drawn to the Catholic Church. I didn't feel completely comfortable signing a statement of faith that the Bible is the only authority. It is certainly the authority, but the tradition and mind of the Church is also an authority in our lives, and helped form the biblical canon. I think I was already Catholic in my heart, but didn't know what to do with that because I hadn't actually joined the Church and wasn't sure I wanted to."

Specifically, Gilbert was drawn to the mysticism of the Eastern Church through reading the works of the Church Fathers, the Desert Fathers of Egypt: the early Christian hermits and ascetics credited with creating the model for Christian monasticism and adherence to prayer, charity and forgiveness. Reading the primary sources, she says, brought the clarity she sought in her spiritual quest.

She was led to the Ukrainian Catholic Church through members of Ottawa's St. John the Baptist Shrine, whom she met while studying at Augustine College. "I remember attending several services, in both Ottawa and Brampton, Ontario, at St. Elias Church, and feeling completely overwhelmed by beauty. The peaceful simplicity of worship was welcome relief from the drums and flashing lights of loud, oftentimes chaotic, Evangelical services. I remember being drawn at the Ukrainian Catholic churches to stand before the icons, these *windows into heaven*, in perplexed wonderment. I heard the chanting of ancient hymns sung by the early Christians as the sun faded, and suddenly felt myself become part of this moving stream of faith that has been ongoing from the beginning of the Church. And, above all, Christ was elevated, perpetually lifted up in spoken prayers, adored in chanted hymns, portrayed in painted icons, revealed in the Holy Scriptures, and manifested fully in the Eucharist itself."

Gilbert, who has a British-French-German background and who previously knew very little about the Ukrainian Catholic Church and understands only a few Ukrainian words, started attending English-language vespers on Saturday evenings and English Divine Liturgy on Sunday mornings at the Shrine. After years of searching for a spiritual home, she finally found it in Canada's capital city in a Ukrainian Catholic church – a tradition and culture that was thoroughly not her own.

"I finally knew I wanted to be received into the Church, and I hoped to do this before I left Ottawa, as opposed to starting a brand-new connection with another faith community," explains Gilbert, who was chrismated at St. John the Baptist on Holy Thursday, April 17, 2014. "I was getting ready to move to a very small town in Kansas of only about 2,000 people, with no Eastern Catholic church close by."

Although it was difficult for them to accept Gilbert's decision to become a Catholic of the Byzantine Ukrainian tradition, her parents flew from South Africa to Ottawa to attend her chrismation on short notice. "There were tears, in private between us, but they were happy that I was not leaving the faith and they met some people from a part of the Church they didn't even know existed," recalls Gilbert. Fr. Peter Galadza, who initially seemed surprised by Gilbert's decision but supported her choice to join the Church, invited her father to deliver the homily, which he did. In Gilbert's opinion, "it was a wonderful sermon."

But while accepting her decision to join the Ukrainian Catholic Church was difficult for Gilbert's parents, it was also a struggle for her that manifested in a profound way two nights before she was to be chrismated. "I had the most tangible sense of being strangled," Gilbert recalls. "I could feel an actual weight on my chest and neck and voices screaming all sorts of strange things, that I was making a mistake, that this was all a lie, that I was entering an empty religion. More than just causing me to question, it was actually really terrifying, as I had never experienced something that oppressive. Needless to say, I did not sleep that night. Somewhat apologetically and embarrassed, I emailed several people for prayer and was advised to read several Psalms, which I did. I slowly gained peace, but it was frightening and unnerving right before my chrismation."

"The chrismation itself was beautiful, and also terrifying in its own way, I suppose. I bought a flimsy white top and skirt at a thrift store – it was definitely not the time to find white warm clothes in the early spring – and remember trembling from being chilled, nervous, excited and confused. I actually didn't fully know what to expect; I stumbled over my confession and the rest of the service. But afterwards, there was just a quiet peace, and a crescendo of joy that continues to bubble up whenever I think back on it."

She says that she felt called to be a Catholic, but still does not fully know why she was led to the Ukrainian Catholic Church. "But I do know that this is where the Lord guided me, and I'm called to be faithful and serve him in whatever way. I've certainly met a lot of wonderful people and grown a lot in my faith through them."

Gilbert also provided some insight into why she joined the Ukrainian Catholic Church in a final paper she wrote at Augustine College, entitled "Reductionism in Church History, Evangelism and Missions: Salvation, Sanctification and the Sacramental Life." In it, Gilbert views her "radical ecclesial shift as a fulfillment of what has been deposited to me by the [Holy] Spirit over the course of my life … rather than a rejection of prior faith or belief."

It has been, she wrote, "a natural movement, an embracing of the holistic (both Catholic and Orthodox) Church. By 'natural,' I do not suggest that this journey was not confusing or painful at times, for myself or for others, nor do I claim now to have a full understanding of what I believe."

"This was a decision that involved both spiritual and mental discernment, if the two can even be separated. Spiritually, this journey was akin to a tumultuous dream, much like the Song of Songs, a woman searching for her lover in the streets, begging the watchmen to know if they had seen him and embracing him when she found him. Like Mary Magdalene, sobbing before the 'gardener' at the empty tomb, she pleaded to know where His Body had been placed, only to be blinded in joy at the sight of Him, alive, in front of her. In the end, I too was astonished, awakened, to find myself in His home, gazing upon His face, as if I had never been anywhere else all along; the confusion faded in His morning light, 'for now we see through a glass, but darkly, and then, face to face!'"

"Entering into communion in the Ukrainian Greco-Catholic Church has since proved to be the most deeply satisfying, spiritually enriching and joyfully sombre place of rest for my soul. It provides both a place of rest and a workshop to strive for holiness, through the liturgical calendar, through the fasts and feasts, through the constant reminder of the need to cultivate an ascetic life in the midst of a chaotic secular environment. Therefore, I am called to prayer, called to fast, called to give."

Given her background in science and medicine, Gilbert acknowledges that she also approached her decision to join the Church analytically. "The most meaningful decisions I make tend to be more along the intuitive. When I know, I know. I *just knew* that I was meant to join the Church at the Ottawa Shrine," explains Gilbert, who holds a certificate in Catholic healthcare ethics from the Philadelphia-based National Catholic Bioethics Center and is now pursuing a master's degree in bioethics at the University of Mary, a private Catholic college in Bismark, North Dakota.

"What led me up to that was definitely processing through, reading through and systematically addressing Catholic Church doctrine through the lens of someone raised in an Evangelical faith community. I also hope to obtain a master's degree in Eastern Christian theology to fill in all of the gaps that I missed."

Besides just book learning, she feels that joining the Ukrainian Catholic Church has enabled her to be a "better Christian, received into a Church filled with martyrs who held fast to the faith during Soviet times and many other hardships. There is a kinship that spreads beyond time and space in the Body of Christ."

"To be a member of the Church and receive the Sacred Mysteries, the sacraments, has been a huge blessing in my life. It opens access for me to be receptive to the Lord in any way that I wanted to be before, but didn't have the means to be within myself," Gilbert explains.

"In a lot of ways, it provides a structure to have prayers that are set for me and to have things that are required of me, such as the Nativity Fast or Lenten Fast as part of the seasons of the Church. It leads me in a way that is good for my soul, whereas previously I somewhat was left to my own devices of trying to figure out what I am going to read in the Bible today, how I am going to pray today, where I want to go to church, and what style of music and décor I most prefer. I don't do these things perfectly. But in my daily life, I strive to have morning and evening prayers using language given to me by the Church – and I have an icon corner in my home. It's a part of my life – and has led me to love better, to serve better and to be a better doctor, I hope."

She also believes that embracing Ukrainian Catholicism has had an effect on the way she practises medicine. "It's a part of the way I try to approach my patients, to see them as icons of Christ, to be mindful of the fact that I'm just as much of a patient as they are in terms of my being 'soul-sick.' There's so much richness in the language of the prayers in the Ukrainian Catholic Church of our desperate need for God's mercy and grace, his forgiveness and healing. We are all ill in many ways, yet we bear Christ's image, and I think that's something that is often lost in the hallways and offices of our daily lives," says Gilbert.

"I also often think of the icon of the Good Samaritan. It is Jesus himself who picks us up, broken and bleeding on the side of the road. He washes us, binds up our wounds and carries us to the innkeeper, which is the Church. We are all equally in need of this true healer of body and soul."

"So I think this informs my practice: that everyone I meet is an icon of Christ and that he is the one who comes to us in our brokenness to restore us to his image. I must strive to think, what would Jesus do in this situation? Do I want to rush in and out to see a patient in a hospital room, or am I willing to just go in and sit next to their bed and listen to them? Do I remain with them in their pain and suffering? I cannot say I'm good at this, but I know it is better medicine, and it's also what Jesus would do. And the theology and imagery of the East makes this easier to remember."

However, for now, Gilbert's connection to the Ukrainian Catholic Church is a private devotion, since there are no churches of this denomination in Wichita, Kansas, where she continues to practice medicine. As of 2017, she has joined the faculty at Via Christi Health – a Catholic-run healthcare provider in Kansas, and the largest in the state – as an assistant clinical professor of the family medicine program run through the University of Kansas.

She regularly attends Mass at a Roman Catholic church in Wichita and vespers at an Antiochian Orthodox cathedral in the city. But there was once a Ukrainian Catholic mission in Kansas' largest urban centre. Gilbert lightheartedly offers: "Perhaps I'm in Wichita to try to get the mission parish started up again!"

"But one day at a time."

7

Joshua Alli-Smith: Finding Beauty in Faith

Joshua Alli-Smith during his baptism on Holy Saturday, with Fr. Michael Winn presiding at St. John the Baptist Ukrainian Catholic Shrine.

Joshua on the front steps of the Shrine after Saturday vespers.

mong Generation Z, Joshua Alli-Smith is a rare gem composed of elements of physical beauty, intellectual dexterity
and spiritual desire. Look at him and you could easily pic-
ture his attenuated six-foot-tall figure walking a runway at Milan
Fashion Week. Listen to him and you could easily imagine the
mocha-skinned model with a British clip morph into an academic
delivering a lecture at the University of Oxford. Speak with Alli-
Smith and you discover a young man passionate about the world
whose search for a deeper meaning of who he is within it led him
to the Ukrainian Catholic Church.

It may not be an unlikely destination for someone of his cosmopolitan background. Born in 1998 in Osaka, Japan, where his
English-born father and his Guyanese-born mother were teaching
English as a second language, Alli-Smith was raised in a multi-faith
and multi-ethnic family. His parents were married in Japan in a
Catholic church. His mother's ancestral roots are in Islam (Alli-
Smith's middle name is Anand, which in Sanskrit means "hap-
piness"), but she was raised in the Lutheran Church, whereas his
father grew up Roman Catholic. Things became more focused on
the religious side when the family moved from Japan to Canada in
2001 and settled in Waterloo, Ontario.

"My mother's family is culturally conservative; she was taken
by the family values of the German Christian community in which
they found themselves after immigrating to Canada and for whom
religion was, in many ways, the fulcrum for everything else," recalls
Alli-Smith. "So we would attend the Mennonite Brethren church
and would sometimes go to an Evangelical Lutheran church, but
my father was unaccustomed to the fundamentalist aspects of it and
didn't want to go – perhaps because of the way North American
Christianity surpasses 'mere' cultural ritual, and has a status in both
the political and scientific dimensions of public life, especially as
something regarded as 'right-wing' and 'intransigent.'"

Alli-Smith says that during this time, he was "wonderfully
immune to the dissension" within his family, and that his interests
lay elsewhere, something arguably natural for someone his age at

the time. "I wanted only to climb trees, go on bike rides and catch frogs – things I would often enjoy doing with my father."

But things would change when his father found work in Ottawa and the family moved to the national capital in 2005. "Living in Ottawa, although no closer to the U.K., did bring us closer to the paternal side of the family, whether over Christmas, or on summer holidays in the Maritime provinces. Reflecting on this, I am grateful especially for the influence my grandmother had on my youth," Alli-Smith recalls, crediting her for shifting some of his focus.

"On one occasion, we were visiting the Church of St. Michael and All Angels in Haworth, Yorkshire, and I was feeling bored," says Alli-Smith. "Here was another old building, I thought, the significance of which was the opinion of people far removed from me, or dead. My grandmother redirected my attention, however, pointing out that the architecture, stained glass and the church as a whole were all meant to provide us 'with a sense of God,' at once tied to our approach to these symbols – our 'posture' in being present in the church – but not intrinsic to it. At the time I scoffed at the suggestion. But she inspired a way of thinking about faith which remained with me."

His voracious appetite for knowledge further shaped his faith journey. Home-schooled throughout his childhood, Alli-Smith ate books whole and was consumed by classical ideas about the meaning of life espoused by great thinkers and writers. The precocious lad was hungry for more, so his parents enrolled him in Augustine College, a private, non-denominational, one-year liberal arts college in Ottawa, where in 2013 he studied philosophy, patristics and the trivium: grammar, logic and rhetoric. There, he met Lisa Gilbert, an American physician with an Evangelical Christian background who was also studying at the college and who would soon join the Ukrainian Catholic Church. The two became fast friends.

In June 2015, Gilbert invited Alli-Smith to Sunday Divine Liturgy at St. John the Baptist Ukrainian Catholic Shrine, where she had been chrismated the year before. "It was all tremendously enrapturing. I felt surrounded by beauty and wanted to have an appreciation for this place rooted in history but very much alive in the present," says Alli-Smith, who had never before attended an Eastern-rite liturgy. "There was a sense of joy – at once purposive and gratuitous – and I wanted to understand this joy for which I had no reference point to draw from my past experience."

"That Sunday also emphasized how intellectually dissatisfying religion had been for me, inasmuch as I had seen it in the years prior, and that here was a holy tradition that I did not understand in full, and did not *need to* in order to participate, or at least not primarily. More clearly than I had seen in the Latin masses that I attended with my grandmother, the onus, or 'quasi-religious duty' to know the propers for the day, to say the right words and display the right emotion – in other words, to '*do Mass*' – passes from a matter of individual effort to participation, and participation in something that is already complete."

"What's primary and more fundamental than this is the disposition of our hearts, and ideally this is absence of necessity in the openness to love. I think this truth is shown best in our love for life, and particularly new life, in our baptism of infants, and their reception of the Eucharist, where their understanding is not a limit to their belonging, both in the community and in the Liturgy."

"It was also the suggestion of a gentleman standing to my right that Sunday," he adds, "to not worry about where we were in the book, but to simply be present and be attentive."

Alli-Smith's liturgical experience at the Shrine resulted in a personal revelation and awareness of a spiritual disjointedness. "I did not know who I was, but I knew who I was not, and had never been: a Protestant Christian. Perhaps I had been thinking too much about my experiences, and feeling too little, because I could not find within myself the desire to identify with people who claimed to have 'found God' amidst the smoke and lights of contemporary 'worship music,' or indeed, any such tradition that spoke of the Divine in terms derived from the basest level of human experience, riddled in simile and emotivism," he explains. "This was a real problem for me, that whatever the worth of religion might be, knowledge of its worth should supposedly depend on my emotional state and rational assent – neither of which I could easily contrive."

"At churches our family had visited, I found that Protestants I engaged with were concerned with things that I thought were, at best, corollary to religious faith itself – in their preoccupation with the here and now, waging war with secularism and its purported rise, and efforts to rack up converts. As heirs to the Reformation, swaths of Christian thought were passed over or given no account, particularly regarding the centrality of sacraments, which is something I noted. This is not to say that Protestantism could never be *helpful*. Sermons were wide-ranging: from how to strengthen your family to how to arrange your finances – faith, or more specifically, the Bible, was the guidebook for life."

Alli-Smith claims the Protestant approach to faith "can easily devolve to the level of the individual's experience and judgment, in their reading of Scripture and opinion of how 'good' the sermon was that day – a level of experience that orthodox Christianity seeks to sublimate and ground within dogma and adherence to sacred tradition."

"In so being a 'help for life' in Protestantism," he explains, "Christianity is made far less about *life unto itself.* But it's a new life, Life *per se,* and a steadfast pursuit of that which was beautifully reified by Christ on the Cross: the truth of what it means to be human."

"In determining what's what," Alli-Smith adds that the question of authority in Protestantism "is never answered otherwise than 'God.' I thought that that 'God' seems so distant when you're thinking about him all the time, for it is you who is thinking it."

"I did engage a few pastors, however, and they were generous with their time. But although I did not then know what I wanted, I knew that their answers wouldn't last me. A certain minister suggested I study theology, it seems, to arrive at 'correct' answers pertaining to, but frustratingly not really found within, the life of that church itself. Realizing this at the time, I was delighted to find a whole tradition within 20th-century Orthodox and Catholic thought that argued that theology is always rooted in doxology, found in the lived experience of the Church stretched out over millennia. People for whom the question of approaching God in faith is not isolated to oneself, or in a spatio-temporal sphere, but essentially the self-same endeavour throughout history – and not only conceptually, but actually."

Alli-Smith was intrigued by Ukrainian Catholicism and began further reading into patristics and other texts on Eastern Christianity. He wanted to know more about the faith but did not want to become a "nominal" Ukrainian Catholic who only attends the liturgy at Christmas and Easter and whose values are "practical at the expense of being substantive." He sought something deeper spiritually and personally.

"I come from a disparate background and a family where we don't get along, due at least in part to the absence of a cohesive religious or cultural heritage, so I've been desirous of stability, peace and clarity about who I am – an identity the Church seemed to offer," he explains candidly.

Alli-Smith began attending the Shrine in January 2016. He also met Fr. Peter Galadza, of the Sheptytsky Institute. Alli-Smith attended vespers at the Institute's chapel and was struck by Galadza's intensity. "I remember him walking from behind the iconostasis swinging a censer with his eyes closed. In him, I found passion without either inhibition or guile, or sometimes even care for fire safety," Alli-Smith says wryly.

Based on his readings, liturgical experiences, intellectual interpretations and friendships with Ukrainian Catholics who, like him, were not of Ukrainian ethnicity, Alli-Smith was persuaded that the community he desired could be found in the Ukrainian Catholic Church. "I didn't see myself anywhere else," says Alli-Smith.

In 2016, he decided he wanted to be baptized a Ukrainian Catholic; he began to prepare for it with the assistance of Fr. Michael Winn, rector of Holy Spirit Ukrainian Catholic Seminary, also situated in Ottawa at the time. Winn prepared a year-long catechesis composed of lectures and readings for Alli-Smith.

"We went through instruction in the faith and history of the Church, and had great discussions and debates," recalls Alli-Smith, who also underwent two emotional minor exorcisms before his baptism. "I recognized that when discussing Christianity, it is similar to, or becomes essentially part of, a speculative philosophy – a coherent, necessary system of ideas within which the vicissitudes of human experience can be contextualized. In other words, it's a theory of everything, but also a lived experience, and therefore not the summation of whatever we may think or say about it. That was particularly appealing to me, in that I do not know all there is to know about life, much less God."

Inwardly focused by nature, Alli-Smith also underwent a process of self-examination. "This introspection was really retrospection. I saw that whatever goals I set, ideals I aspired to or standards others expect me to meet, I don't always meet them and make the cut. I'm always falling short of perfection, and to do this is nothing less than sin," he says. "I think that within the Church, there isn't so much a rule book for what not to do as a positive prescription and orientation toward virtue and what is good. Despite this, I did sort of stumble through Holy Week, feeling far more uncertain of my commitment than a year prior, because I saw myself more clearly than before as someone undeserving of the good that baptism represented."

Alli-Smith's baptism, held at St. John the Baptist during the Paschal Vigil on Holy Saturday 2017, found him diving into his new spiritual home. Dressed in black (his favourite colour) from head to toe, Alli-Smith was thrice immersed by Winn into a plastic wading pool placed at the front of the church. Following this, Alli-Smith donned a white robe made by Winn's mother, Gloria Romaniuk Winn. "I felt an almost overwhelming sense of calm," recalls Alli-Smith, who adopted the baptismal name Theophan. "All of my internal self-doubts, which had engulfed me only moments before, disappeared, and it was a new birth – in the death of my old life. I was also clearly aware of what had been done for me: it was very much the faith and efforts of others that carried me to Pascha."

It was a time when he also remembered his grandmother's influence on his life. "I think that my conversion came as a surprise to her when I emailed her a few days before my baptism. It wasn't anticipated, much less something she had intended to influence me toward. But it was her gentle, unassuming relationship to me that gave me cause to consider the worth of her tradition from which she drew so much peace," he recalls.

"Memorably, on my 17th birthday, she wished me well on all my pursuits and wrote: 'We could spend a lifetime in our search for truth, but even with limited knowledge, such as I have, we should always endeavour to live rightly, and help others to do the same by our example. This is to search after God.'"

Yet Alli-Smith's search continues. "This may be strange to readers of a book about people who have converted to a religion, but I do not know that I have faith, or at least I do not know that I know God," says Alli-Smith. "It isn't that my reasons for joining the Church aren't discernible. In other words, that I do not know why I was baptized, or what life after that would entail, but that the presuppositions that led me to faith were derived entirely from my own experience – the people I've met, the books I've read, and the liturgies I've been present within – and I cannot know them to be true apart from my own judgment, which I do not trust."

"The experience of reason is that of a double-edged sword, and tends equally well toward the justification of belief as to unbelief. This results in antinomies, paradoxes of truth, where we find equally cogent arguments, say, for the existence of God, but also the negation thereof."

"But I recognize what faith is in its innermost structure, as something a-rational, and that revels in antimony in its catholicity. This understanding provides some solace, in spite of myself. Faith is concerned with things that are by no means 'certain,' and that our intellect cannot adequately divulge, but that reason can provide the groundwork for in necessitating, as an end for all our efforts after living a 'good life.'"

"So I still desire faith, as I did prior to baptism – which allows for, from the perspective of reason alone, at least the possibility of Truth beyond my idea of truth, and, if there is to be any substantive meaning to the word, the God beyond my conception of god. Without this understanding, I think I'd find myself in the existentialism of, say, [Jean-Paul] Sartre. He believed in a 'god-shaped hole' in the human heart, and chose to despair that it can ever be filled – in a way, dogmatically committing himself to one side of an antinomy, with no allowance for doubt."

"This would be a conceptually stagnant position to take, so I'm not into it. As Sartre concluded, in a world without God, the only truth is that 'anything goes.' Generally put, I think the legacy of most 20th-century philosophy confirms this fruitlessness, in the nihilism or moral relativism so often packaged within a fashionable atheism. But atheism is probably a more difficult choice than modern people think."

Moreover, Alli-Smith, who is gay, but committed to living a chaste life, notes that he is alone as an individual within the parish community at St. John the Baptist. "This is a struggle, too. Everyone is either in a relationship or part of a family, and that means I'm different," he explains. "And I don't know that many people very well." But although he does not speak or understand much Ukrainian, he has volunteered every summer at the annual Capital Ukrainian Festival held on the grounds of the Shrine.

Finding a fit within the Church is part of the journey of a young man searching for meaning and purpose in the world. Growing up in southern Ontario, Alli-Smith initially wanted to be a farmer. "I loved the open air, and love animals and vegetables – but I had this desire without knowing much about such work," he says, noting that he understood the "grungy" work only after taking a landscaping job in 2016. "It tired me out and was such a dead weight on the mind, so I don't think farming is for me after all," explains Alli-Smith, who is pursuing an undergraduate honours degree in philosophy at Dominican University College in Ottawa. "At least for the time being, I'm a city slicker."

"Politics are very intriguing, as are philosophy and history, and they all draw from one another, so I'd like to find myself doing something in an intersection of the three."

As for being a Ukrainian Catholic, his wishes are highly personal. "In brief, I want to be happy and have clarity about everything," he says. "I believe that the Church provides me with a framework in which this is at least possible. I continue to have every reason to be a Ukrainian Greco-Catholic, and every reason not to be. But my decision to enter the Church was itself momentous, and so I must appreciate that, and strive to be consistent with it in the present moment – to be a proper Kantian, and a better Christian for it," he offers wryly. "This has yet to be seen, of course, but perhaps that's why the regulative status of religion [in Kantianism] is so crucial. I need to be further regulated!"

"I am reminded often of those words we sing within the Cherubicon, prior to the Great Entrance at the Byzantine Liturgy: 'Now let us lay aside all cares of life, that we may receive the King of all.' Having then sung this with the parish, I think to myself, 'From where else does our preoccupation with certainty, with the justification of belief, and even for the very category of truth arise but from our mundane condition?' – and how much more beautiful liturgy and faith are because of this! The absolution of our earthly cares."

Alli-Smith acknowledges that he still has "a lot left to become." "It seems to me that maturity has a lot to do with balancing self-interest with seeking the best interests of others, usually characterized as charity or love. I want to be everything I ought to be – successful, and yes, I want to love. I have no more immediate examples of how in practice this is possible than my godparents. And to a lesser degree, the saints, the great cloud of witnesses who, I am told, pray unceasingly for our best. To date, and in my life, there has been a no more accessible option to express and be adamant about this desire than that of the Ukrainian Greco-Catholic Church." He adds: "I do not want to be a tourist. I want to be a citizen of the city of God, and the Church. So we'll see what the future holds, and I believe I'll play a part in it. I'd rather be grateful for this part, than – over what it might be worth – skeptical."

"Lord, I believe, but help my unbelief."

8

Landon Coleman:
A Musician Who Struck
the Right Chord

Landon and Lara Coleman and family wait for
the blessing of Paschal foods at St. John the Baptist Shrine.

Landon and his guitar.

Playing music and working with people facing life's challenges have been Landon Coleman's passion for much of his adult life. But the fresh-faced Alberta native spent years trying to find the right chord and connection to give his life meaning and purpose at a spiritual level.

Coleman, who was born in 1986 in the northern Alberta city of St. Albert, near Edmonton, was raised in a long-standing Bible-reading Baptist family. At the age of 14, he was baptized in the Christian and Missionary Alliance, and for five months following high school, attended an Evangelical college in New Zealand.

Based on his faith pedigree, the family expectation was that Coleman would live out his days as a Baptist. His artistic soul wasn't as sure. Music put him on a path to a career. An accomplished bassist, Coleman has performed across Canada as a solo artist and with groups reflecting disparate musical styles, from jazz and bluegrass to rock, country, Celtic and folk. He has also worked as a music therapist, providing therapy sessions for children with special needs, seniors experiencing dementia, and people in hospice care. The artistic caregiver has also recorded a digital album, entitled *Single Life*, released in 2011.

That personal status did not last long. In 2012, the tall and handsome musician married a beautiful historian, Lara, a Roman Catholic, with whom he has three children: William, born in 2014; Edith, born the year after; and Patrick, appropriately born on March 17, 2019.

Coleman followed his heart to find love and a vocation. But on the big questions of life and its meaning, he relied on his mind and searched for answers through reading books. "I wanted to understand big ideas and listen to people who knew something about life," he explains. "Yet the people I kept encountering in books were super-smart and didn't have any time for religion – and certainly no time for Evangelical Christianity, which from my experience didn't seem to care about big questions or ideas."

Coleman, who uses his mother Anne's maiden name, was drawn to a new literary perspective indirectly via his father, Lowell

Riemer, a dentist and a member of the U.S.-based Christian Medical and Dental Associations (CMDA). One of the speakers at a conference the CMDA held in Alberta in the mid-2000s was John Patrick, a retired British-born physician who established Augustine College, a one-year liberal arts college that opened in Ottawa in 1997, and serves as its president.

Coleman, who graduated in 2004 with a diploma in jazz performance from what was then Grant MacEwan College (now MacEwan University) in Edmonton, decided to check out the speaker's presentation. But he also checked out Augustine College's website and was blown away by the reading list posted: it included such classic and timeless titles as Plato's *Republic*, St. Augustine's *Confessions* and St. Thomas Aquinas' *Summa Theologica*.

"I thought if someone could guide me and force me to read this stuff, with a lot of history and big ideas, that it would help me understand something about life at least," explains Coleman, who also, like many of his Evangelical "bookish Christian" friends, also read C.S. Lewis.

"Throughout high school, my friends and I were reading the great books of the 20th century – modern American stuff. But after high school, I liked Tolstoy and Dostoyevsky and knew there was good stuff in non-modern literature; it didn't have to be new to be interesting."

In 2007, he enrolled in Augustine College, where he studied the history of philosophy, art, music, science and the Church, as well as Latin and the trivium: grammar, logic and rhetoric. "There was a lot to chew on," says Coleman. Hungry for a menu of more literary ideas, he used a year and a half of academic credits he received from Augustine to pursue an undergraduate honours degree in English literature at St. Francis Xavier University in Antigonish, Nova Scotia. He focused on Flannery O'Connor, the late American writer and essayist whose works reflected her Roman Catholicism in its examination of morality and ethics.

Coleman found himself reflecting on his own spirituality, but was still uncertain as to which path to follow in finding answers to lingering questions on faith and redemption. After his graduation from St. FX in 2010, he returned to Ottawa – and Augustine College – where he took a job as their recruitment officer. As it turned out, Coleman found himself recruited too. He was invited to attend a "Bring-a-Friend-to-Vespers" service at the Eastern Catholic Chaplaincy pastored by Fr. Peter Galadza, situated in a room within Sacré-Coeur, a Roman Catholic parish on the University of Ottawa campus.

At the time, Coleman was attending Ecclesiax, an emerging-church community in Ottawa for what he describes as "disaffected Evangelicals." Ecclesiax was keen on blending art and music with service to others. "But it fizzled out before my eyes," he recalls. "The pastor had a confrontation with one of the parishioners during a service. It was a total disaster."

Homeless for worship, Coleman was curious about the incense and iconostasis that greeted him at the Chaplaincy vespers. "I first thought it was really interesting, yet strange," he says. "From what I remember, I didn't like it. I couldn't imagine that there was anywhere else in the city where people were in a dark room with a bearded guy in sparkly dress – which I later learned were vestments – with a censer and smoke and candles and these weird icons, and people singing together for an hour. This was an organized strangeness that I had never encountered before. It seemed like it didn't belong in the modern world."

The "bearded guy" was Galadza, who would play a pivotal role in leading Coleman to answers regarding his questions on faith. Coleman would see Fr. Peter again when he was invited to attend a Sunday morning English-language Divine Liturgy at the Chaplaincy. "The liturgy was attractive to me," explains Coleman. "I almost immediately realized that it was amazing that God was working there, that there was something going on."

"When the congregation sang the Beatitudes – I had never heard them sung before in my life – it was beautiful. I had just come from attending an Evangelical church where the people were singing how great they felt because God loved them. It was sometimes quite a superficial, feeling-based approach to worship."

"Part of my being disaffected with the Evangelical Church had been the 'feeling' stuff – that worship was based on how they felt about God. Well, guess what, I know a lot of people who are having a terrible time and don't feel like singing about how so-in-love they are with God – these proclamations of love and devotion. And I was a 20-year-old where there were a lot of things going on in my life and in my friends' lives that were not going well."

"I knew God existed, and I was pretty sure he is good. But it didn't inspire me to clap my hands and dance around. I always thought: Why don't these people in worship just say things they know are true? If they know that God is good, why not sing about that?"

Coleman then attended St. John the Baptist Shrine. He liked what he heard there. "It didn't matter how you felt: there was this beautiful, true stuff – the Beatitudes, the Our Father being sung. I thought, this has the power to change a person. There was so much care taken in the liturgy. People were trying hard to make things look and sound beautiful. They focused on giving the best that humanity can give to God. It didn't seem like it was stuck in 2007, like modern worship music is very much in the moment."

"If you get a Christian who's really listening and really praying with people in an Eastern Church, how could they say no to it? What we are praying is the substance of faith."

Coleman credits Andrew Bennett, who shifted from Roman Catholicism to Ukrainian Catholicism and was ordained a deacon in 2017, with helping explain the faith to him. "I remember asking him about the Eucharist, and he said it was the body and blood of Jesus. And I told him that growing up an Evangelical, we talked about it as being a commemoration of the Last Supper. And Andrew said, "No, the host and the wine *is* Jesus."

Coleman was also experiencing what he describes as a cognitive dissonance between how he was supposed to act, based on his faith background, and what he was supposed to believe.

"I recall talking with a Roman Catholic who wanted to know more about my background in Evangelicalism. When I told him that I grew up not drinking, he was appalled – and I think I know why. On the one hand, no one in my house drank, and on the other hand, in college I was having good meaningful conversations with friends over pints. Also, we were supposed to be glorifying God with our prayer services, and yet I had had more profound experiences of beauty and meaning in music outside of church."

"What I wanted, and I wrote this in a journal at the time in early 2007, was 'some sort of unifying idea' – a 'mantra' that would bring together the bits of my Christian belief and experience together with my gut feelings about peace, my experiences of gratitude and beauty, of joy and friendship. I wanted something to follow rather than create."

In mid-January 2008, Coleman attended the Theophany celebration at the Canadian Museum of History, across the river from Ottawa in Gatineau, Quebec. He remembers what he experienced and what he felt that day. "There in the softly falling snow, the choir sang beside a big ice cross and a priest blessed the Ottawa River and all the waters in the world. It was beautiful, though a bit alienating, and strange. Afterward, there was a party at someone's house that I was invited to. The thing I remember most vividly was a bearded Orthodox deacon, who arrived in his cassock with a bottle of vodka. He poured shots for everyone and yelled 'Christ is baptized!' and we all did a shot together. Now this was something, I thought. Finally, a reason to drink! A reason to celebrate! And a good reason that Christ has somehow, by entering our water, sanctified the whole natural world, restoring its goodness and divinity. I could get behind this sort of bodily, lived religious experience: not cut off from everyday life or the body, but felt. And Easter that year was the same way. I decided to do my best with eating vegan during Lent, and not drinking. But when Easter came, I knew there was a reason to feast. After 40 days of that, my body wanted meat and cheese and eggs and beer, and my heart wanted it! All of me wanted to kiss the other members of the parish at Agape Vespers on Easter Sunday afternoon and sing 'Christ is risen!' And I could see on their faces that they were, in fact, happier there – singing and eating and drinking because Christ had beaten death – than they were about a good financial portfolio or a promotion at work. This sincerity in pursuing a unified life was and still is so compelling to me."

Coleman experienced similar great emotion on a more sombre occasion on the Church calendar when he first attended Forgiveness Vespers later in 2008. "That name might not ring a bell for some Ukrainian Catholics, but it is a shame because it is a tradition that needs to be rediscovered," he explains. After singing a short vespers service on the eve of Great Lent, the priest stands at the front of the church with every community member in single file forming a line ending with him. "When I attended the service at St. John the Baptist Shrine, the priest – Fr. Galadza – stood facing the first person in line, which in this case was his wife, Olenka. She said to him, 'Forgive me,' and she lay prostrate, forehead to the ground, in front of him. He then said to her, 'I forgive you and God forgives,' and then said, 'Forgive me,' and fell to the ground before her. It ended with an embrace. She then stood beside him and each person in the community asked for and extended forgiveness to every other person."

"Little kids and old men, brothers and sisters, husbands and wives, old friends did this. There were lots of tears, and I remember thinking, 'I don't know these people very well, this might be awkward,' and so I told Andrew Bennett how I was feeling. Andrew said, 'Landon, you think your sin only affects you? You think your sin doesn't affect each of the people in this room?' He left me with that. And while that first year was awkward, my experience of asking forgiveness and forgiving those people that I would eventually sit on committees with and would occasionally jostle with in the course of parish and family life has been life-giving. I cry like a baby every year."

What drew Coleman to join the Ukrainian Catholic Church when he was chrismated at St. John the Baptist in the summer of

2008 was its "embodied spirituality: not this list of things to believe, but rather a bunch of people doing stuff that shows what they believe. They don't just believe that God is present in some abstract way in their Church, but that he is present in the Eucharist. They go so far as to bow their foreheads to the ground to show that they believe that."

"It was the opposite of what I ended up with in the Evangelical tradition. In the church I went to in high school, you just wore jeans to church, nothing special. God is everywhere and he loves you the way you are, which I think is fair. But people do dress up for important things, so this idea of acting out belief rather than just saying it was compelling to me."

He credits Galadza as "the perfect person" to introduce him to the Ukrainian Catholic Church. "He means every word of the liturgy that he says and takes all of the traditions seriously," explains Coleman, who will also always remember when Galadza chrismated him on August 29, 2008. "I had to say the Nicene Creed out loud, and it felt like being alone on the edge of a precipice. But it also felt good – it felt like a turning point. I had seen the fruits of people believing and acting on those words."

He acknowledges that it is not always easy to be a believer. "Ottawa is a tough town, and there aren't a lot of people my age who are churchgoers, so I sometimes feel like a weirdo." However, since his chrismation, Coleman has become more comfortable identifying as a Ukrainian Catholic. "I used to say I was an Eastern Christian living in the West in communion with Rome. Now that I'm involved on parish council at St. John the Baptist as the pro-life committee representative and help run the youth group at the parish, I am now also indebted to Ukrainian culture for carrying along its traditions. I realize that the first people I need to be serving are Ukrainian Camdians," says Coleman, who is of German, French, Irish and British background, and does not speak Ukrainian. "The process of becoming Ukrainian Catholic was quick. But the process of learning to be Ukranian Catholic in a productive way and to contribute to the community is going to be lifelong."

A former Evangelical, he now hopes to play an evangelizing role at the Shrine by helping to attract other non–Ukrainian Canadians to join the parish. "I want Ukrainians to know that what they have is beautiful and should be shared – and that there has to be a balance struck between preserving the traditions and looking outward to try to make it easy for people to enter if they want to. I'm hopeful that our community will become strong and that we will get some of the non-attending Ukrainian Catholics back to church and minister to non-Ukrainians as well," says Coleman.

"I think a lot of people would fall in love with the aesthetic of the Ukrainian Catholic Church; they may be looking for the rhythm of feasting and fasting, a community that comes with a liturgy that is chockfull of theology that magnifies the mysteries of existence. I think many people want a quiet space that comes with vespers, and people want a Church that is similar to another major religion, Judaism, with the reading of the Psalms and the chanting," Coleman explains.

"I love this church, and I believe its appeal is massive. It's a treasure that shouldn't be hidden."